Saints, Sinners & Angels

STORIES OF PEOPLE; IMAGES OF GOD

Danny Unrau

Winnipeg, Manitoba, Canada   KINDRED PRODUCTIONS   Hillsboro, Kansas, USA

Kindred Productions is the publishing arm for the Board of Resource Ministries of the General Conference of Mennonite Brethren Churches. Kindred publishes, promotes, and markets print and mixed media resources that help shape our Christian faith and discipleship from the Mennonite Brethren perspective.

Saints, Sinners & Angels

Published simultaneously by Kindred Productions, Winnipeg, Manitoba R2L 2E5 and Kindred Productions, Hillsboro, Kansas, USA.

Book design: Fred Koop, Winnipeg, MB
Cover design: Eclectic Fine Arts, Winnipeg, MB
Printed by Christian Press, Winnipeg, MB

Canadian Cataloguing in Publication Data

Unrau, Danny, 1950-

Saints, sinners and angels

ISBN 0-921788-39-8

1. Image of God.   2. God - Knowableness
3. Spiritual life - Christianity   I. Title

BT102.U573   1997   231   C97-920052-0

International Standard Book Number: 0-921788-39-8

For a Free Catalog of Kindred Productions books
Call 1-800-545-7322

Dedication

In memory of my dad, Jacob F. Unrau,
a man who had a wide open window to other people.

1912-1994

Contents

Acknowledgements

I would like to thank all those people who, over the years, asked, "Have you ever thought of writing a book?" Your kind words were incentives that got me and kept me writing when I couldn't get motivated myself. The good people of the two specific congregations I have served as preacher/storyteller, as well, who so attentively let me "test" most of these stories, deserve huge thanks. As do Michael Dick and David Wiebe, for getting me going on this project. Marilyn Hudson and her people for their incredible work, and Arthur Block for his interest, his positive prodding and his concrete encouragement.

I am hugely indebted to all the people who walk through the pages of this book, for they "gifted" me with themselves and, in so doing, allowed me to let their stories become a part of mine. Most importantly, "Thank you!" to Lois, my best friend, who many nights goes to sleep with the light still on and the computer keys clicking away in a house that would otherwise be dark and silent and easier to sleep in. I am too fragile to have done this without her many ways of cheering me on.

Introduction

The stories in this collection are all true. The conversations are as I remember them. Sometimes I have changed names to protect the identity of the innocent, but always I have thought the story better as it happened than it would have been had I invented it.

I have written about this collection of people, these saints and sinners, hoping to remind myself and to tell the readers that the image of God, resident in all his creations, is waiting, waiting to reflect the Creator to all who would but stop and look and listen for him, regardless of how jaded or lost the image-bearer may have become. We live in a world that has become neurotically obsessed with beautiful people, self-made; the Kingdom of God, however, I suspect, is made up of lovable losers on the lookout to be remade by God. Jesus showed his affection to, and was best seen by, those who were unhinged enough to know that they would need God to do something beautiful for them; they could not do it themselves.

I rejoice in the journey to discover my God whom I refer to in this work using the traditional masculine pronoun, though I wish in no way to restrict our view of God to the limitations of our human sexuality. God is not limited by gender; God is beyond being male or female.

God has been revealed to me by this motley gallery of characters you are about to meet. I hope that somewhere someone is encouraged to celebrate each and every person that God puts in his or her way, for all the people we encounter, I am convinced, are in our paths as an opportunity to see just a little of God. The Kingdom, we have been told, is for those with eyes to see and ears to hear. I introduce you to these saints, sinners and angels. Who knows - their designations may be interchangeable.

Author

D anny L. Unrau , usually known as Dan, lives in Rich-
mond, B.C., a suburb of Vancouver, with his wife,
Lois, and their children: Shoshanna, Aila and Levi.
The art of storytelling, so evident in this book, is a
vital part of his life, in and around the church and out into his
community.

Currently the senior pastor of the Fraserview Mennonite
Brethren Church, Dan has pastored for thirteen years, taught
school, worked in construction and sawmilling, been an Immi-
gration officer, and travelled to many corners of the world.

Saints, Sinners and Angels is his first book and is the product of
his interactions in church settings and beyond, a year as a Mennonite Central Committee volunteer in Germany, as a graduate
student in Jerusalem, and his eighteen years growing up on a
farm in rural Manitoba.

Dan's giftedness and insight extend beyond his career and
home church to his active participation on governing boards at
the denominational level.

Looking for Laughter

The Berliner

It was the tenth anniversary of the Berlin Wall. I climbed one of those lonely wooden towers built on the western side to afford the curious the opportunity to look over into the bleakness of East Berlin. A few people milled about around the tower, a few more stood on top with binoculars trained on something or someone on the other side.

Up on the highest level of the tower, at the top of the zigzag stairway, I saw a gentleman - all German, tweed coat jacket, green hat, thick woolen trousers, shiny shoes - talking to a youngish man holding a microphone. A TV camera, NBC emblazoned on its side, recorded the conversation. I crowded in to hear the story to satisfy my curiosity. The journalist and the interpreter wrapped up the story, and the cameraman swung the camera off his shoulder. I moved closer to the elderly German gentlemen who seemed too stimulated to be finished, too agitated to leave the tower. He must have sensed the energy of my curiosity as he grabbed me by the arm and started into his story.

"See that woman across there? There! Walking arm in arm with that younger woman? That's my wife. The older one. Do you see her? Look!"

"Yes, I see her."

"She's my wife. Like many others ten years ago we lived in East Berlin, but I worked in West Berlin. The day the soldiers rolled out the barbed-wire and the workmen started to build this cursed wall between east and west, I knew it would be dangerous for me to go home again. I had been too vocally anti-Communist. I knew I would not last long with this hammer coming down. I didn't go home that day they built the wall.

"For ten years now I have not talked with my wife. I have not touched her. Almost every day I climb this tower and she walks back and forth on the other side. I wave to her, and she sneaks looks at me, pretending to the border guards and their dogs and guns that she does not notice me. It's not safe for her. Oh no!"

"For ten years you've been climbing this tower and waving to your wife who has been walking back and forth fifty meters away from you, pretending not to see you?"

"Yes! Yes!" he shouted. "But last week she turned sixty-five and I received a phone call. From my wife. How she got my phone number? Her voice was older but it was her. My wife!"

He grinned, tears flowing down his cheeks. His one hand held my hand, the other grasped my arm. He turned back towards the Wall and looked over at his kerchiefed wife strolling back and forth beyond the cement impediment topped with broken bottles. He pointed out the razor-rolls of fence wire, twenty feet or so of mined open space, hungry-looking dogs running back and forth in their confined channels, and the frightening towers and binoculared guards with ready rifles. He raised his hands, cupped his mouth to shout to his wife, but then lowered his hands, saying nothing, and wept.

"I cannot risk it now," he sobbed. "She has such a beautiful voice. And she talked to me on the phone. 'Hans' she said, 'I am coming to you. With sixty-five they will let me out to be with you. I am coming to you.'

"'When? When?' I had shouted. But she did not know. Maybe a week from today. Maybe sooner. I should wait. 'And keep pretending on the tower that you don't know me,' she said. Keep pretending! How do I keep pretending? What if I have a heart attack now and die in the days before she gets here? What if they change their minds? What if this is a trick? What if they have seen me wave to her too often? What if....?"

He searched my face for answers. An elderly German man with too much pain, with too many stories of sorrow, and a huge new hope for tomorrow, hanging on to a long-haired, hitchhiking, spoiled kid from Canada whose worst problem had been a little hunger once or twice and having to sleep by the side of the road in the rain a couple of times, must have been a startling picture of contrast for the NBC news crew.

Bruce Cockburn, the insightful Canadian songwriter/singer, screamed out his wish to have a rocket-launcher when he saw the war injustices of Latin America, so that whoever was responsible for all this horror would have to pay. I confess that when I saw the Berlin Wall for the first time, I wished for a personal jet fighter to strafe the Wall and blow it out of the heart of Berlin. So much did it seem that if only we could get that wall removed, people could be together. It wasn't long before I realized that I was fantasizing a violent solution to a violent situation, and the contradiction in that wish shocked me, shamed me, and saddened me. It left me feeling powerless and hopeless not only about the Wall, but even about myself.

This ache of separation is known to all of us down deep. Why was it so strong standing on that tower, looking over the Wall and watching a husband and a wife relating to each other, so far away from each other, so close together?

God is a reconciler. He wants us put back together. We are Humpty Dumpties who have fallen off the wall, and all the king's horses and all the king's men cannot put us together again. But God can. We are chips off the divine block of God, floating around somewhat independently but forlornly without him. He wants us back. He throws out the lifeline, his son's death, to us, but he lets us decide whether we want to grasp onto him and come back.

I feel important, I feel good, when somebody wants to be with me. Imagine the sensation when I grasp the idea that God, the Creator, wants to be with me. God wants him and me intimately connected. Reconciled is what the Bible calls it.

How do we get reconciled with God? How do we get the walls down? How do we get the stories together, the people together, so that those with too much pain get some relief, and those with too little can get some reality? How do we tell the world that God sent his son to die on the cross for us so that there would never be a Berlin Wall between God and us? How do we exude that wall-lessness that will make people want to tug at the corners of our garments and ask us about our God? How will we stop being so dour about God having saved us and just start dancing it and shouting it?

"Tumbling Down" shouted the newspapers. "Chipping away" sang Crosby, Stills, and Nash. And down came the hated Berlin Wall. Did you see the dancing, celebrating people? Can you imagine the party if our world could see that the Berlin Wall was an easy thing compared to the Wall of sin in each of us, and that Jesus, the God-Man, is waiting, waiting, waiting to smash down with his love?

It feels so good to live without a wall down my center; it is so good to live without a wall down our center. He, our God, has washed it away in red blood, and we are sparkling clean and whole and ready to walk with God, forever.

Karl

A fter they dropped me off at a gas station that survives between the opposing flows of the Autobahn and waved "good-bye", I waited for my hosts alone. A gray Opel came out of the hills, down through the underpass, gained the lane between the screaming super highway and pulled up beside me. A youngish thirty with a broad smile and a friendly handshake shouted the greeting question,

"Den? Den?"

"Yes," I said, "I'm Dan. Are you Walter?"

We drove into the hills along winding roads. My inner compass needle was twirling, shifting directions, getting lost. Soon I knew I couldn't go home even if I wanted to. I wouldn't know which way to go.

Around a curve through calendar-like scenery with the smells of summer grass and sweetish village barnyard manure piles wafting in through the open car window and up and into a courtyard, the Opel stopped with a squeak. We were surrounded on three sides by a high two-story edifice, tile roofed, one wing house, another wing barn. I heard soon that the *Hof,* the yard, the main building, was 300 years old.

They put running water into my room for my convenience, thinking that North Americans couldn't live without a sink in their room. I didn't tell them that we only got indoor plumbing and central heating in our farm home eight years ago. I forgot. I went to sleep that night, desperately lonely, under a feather blanket so thick and heavy I couldn't move. In the morning I heard singing outside in the courtyard.

I couldn't see anyone through my window, so I followed the sound of the cracking voice out the door and across the cobblestone pavement. There he was. A little man covered with dust, sitting on the bottom step of a rough wooden stairway. He was dressed in blue. Blue sweat pants were stuffed into the tops of black, orange-trimmed rubber boots. Above the waistband of his sweat pants, I could see the waistband of at least two more pairs of the same thickness trousers. This man was thickly dressed. His heavily-buttoned woolen sweater speckled with straw and more than a little dirt, open at the neck, showed two or three shirts layered below the first. A blue shapeless hat made of paper, with a thin yellow plastic visor, and the name CLUB emblazoned above it, all floated on a mass of rakish black hair that looked like it hadn't been washed in months. Between the hat and the array of collars, the face. An unforgettable face. Eyes sunken deeply into greatly wrinkled sockets, but eyes, in spite of their yellowish hue and severe bloodshotness, that sparkled when they could finally focus on me. I sensed immediately that this drunken singer was a delightful person. His mouth owned no teeth, and his nose flattened, askew and cartilage free like the nose of a wizened, retired New York boxer, was red and purple and veined and bulbous. His whole face was a semi-pudgy mass of caved-in purple hues. Worry-lines, laugh lines, ran away from his eyes. His eyebrows and his cheeks hid his eyes when he smiled and when he laughed. His hands were as misshapen as his nose and just as purple. The fingers were crooked and stiff, apparently semi-paralyzed. His legs were bowed and unsteady, even in sitting.

Suddenly, the singer tried to get up but couldn't. Finally, he just reached out his hand to shake mine. The hand was weak, and it was cold. It felt dead. A pungent smell, reminiscent of what exudes from chicken barns, wafted from my new friend and drifted toward me. There's a perfume out called Poison; the smell coming at me was what I would have thought some poisons must smell like.

"*Alte* Karl!" He said, "I am old Karl. And I am useless. Good to meet you. Do you know, '*Du, Du liegst mir im herzen*'?" And he started singing again.

He nearly fell off his perch on the step. He coughed, awfully, like a volcano about to erupt, swore, and waved his hand as if to say, "What's the use anyway! Forget it!"

"Are you the American?" he asked, squinting, trying to get a clearer view of me than his eyes were probably capable of.

"Yes, well, I am Canadian," I answered. He grinned and wiped some spittle off his chin with the back of his woolened wrist. It wasn't the first time that wrist band had been used as a face wiper.

"I was in the war," he started, eyes suddenly seeming far away. "I saw the Eiffel Tower. Climbed it! Do you want to see my problem? My sickness?"

Over the next few months Karl became a friend. Sort of. Once a month he received his army pension. It took him eight days to drink it. And during those eight days we never saw him sober; we never got him to work, or eat. Twice in six months he gave me his money on the first day the mailman brought it and made me promise not to give it to him no matter what. When he came begging for it a few days later, I said, "No!" and reminded him that he had instructed me to not give it to him. He, in turn, reminded me that it was his money and he would charge me with theft if I didn't give it to him. So I gave it to him. He got drunk again until the money was all gone.

Sober, though, Karl was delightful. Charming. Funny. He was a lovable loser whom everyone in the neighborhood knew, everyone liked.

For a whole year Karl tried to walk to a larger

town in the next valley from our home village to get the denturist to fit him with false teeth. He never once made it past the pub in the first village. The last time I saw him, Karl still had no teeth.

Once he came to me with a noosed rope ready to hang himself. I talked him out of it, though I must confess, I did wonder what I would have to hope for if I were looking at life through his eyes. In the aftermath of that event, Karl told me that life really wasn't that difficult. "You just have to understand it," he said. I wonder if Karl is still living; I wonder if he ever really understood.

Karl's eyes sparkled when he talked of the war. And he talked of the war every day. I soon came to understand that it was only during the war that he felt much worth as a human being. For all of the horror we remember of Hitler, and I shudder at seeing anything positive in this man or what he ever did, he did infuse a whole generation of German folk with a sense of worth, a vision of greatness, and a reason for hope.

We hope we will do well in school. We hope our parents won't get divorced. We hope we get a job. We hope we will get married. We hope the child will be healthy and normal. We hope that the kids find God. We hope that death won't be painful. We hope. We hope. We hope.

Faith, Hope, and Love, and the greatest is love. But of these, what is hope? Knowing God is hope. Hope is the ability to keep going when it's too hard to go any further. Hope is the courage to stand tall when it feels like no one else is standing. Hope is the commitment to say what must be said even though it will probably get us into trouble. Hope is the energy to try again. Hope is the strength to hear cutting soul-killing criticism but refusing to quit.

I know people who buy 6-49 tickets in the hope that they might win, but live in the terror of what might happen if they did. I know people who do stupid things because they have no hope; they think they have nothing to lose. But I also know people who live with an abundance of hope because they have been touched by God. That's the way God is. He touches the hopeless with hope.

He gave hope to people in the Russian Gulag. He gave hope to people in boxcars and steamships traveling to a new country with no money in their pockets. He gave hope when the dust storms and the markets wiped out the new beginnings. And he gives hope when it seems all that matters now is money and success. God engenders hope. He renews people. The tired, the sick, the hungry, the angry, the crazy. He can get people so high that they rise like eagles. He can help people to run and run and run, and amazingly, not get tired. He can enable people to walk, softly and slowly, but without stopping, without getting too tired to go on. We aren't always able to soar and hit the heights, and we aren't always able to run tirelessly, but with God inside us, beside us, in back of us, out in front of us, above us, before us, we can know that we will always be able to keep going. Life can never serve us too much. That's what hope is. That's who God is.

Whether old Karl ever grasped God's hope that reached out to him or not, I don't know. But old Karl, useless Karl, didn't need to live without hope. He was not too far gone for God. No one ever is. God was not incapable of giving Karl every reason to live. If Karl could smile. If Karl can find a reason. There must be hope. There must be God.

Herbert

He threatened to kill me with a pitchfork. We, Herbert, the hired man, and I, were cleaning the chicken barns. Herbert was ranting and raving about Walter who, again, he said, had not given him a day off as he had been promised. Herbert clearly had forgotten that yesterday he had put on his town clothes, walked to the gate, stopped, turned around, come back, put on his work clothes, climbed up onto the Massey Ferguson and spent the day ploughing the top field. Not yet recognizing nor even faintly understanding Herbert's logic, or lack of it, I mumbled something that if he didn't like working for Walter, why didn't he just quit and go somewhere else. My comment touched a button somewhere deep in Herbert's madness. He aimed the shiny tangs of his pitchfork between my chest and my throat, and as he roared, I think for an instant, I knew how the harp-playing David felt about dodging flying spears. Herbert didn't throw the fork nor bury its tangs between my ribs that day, but I learned in that, abruptly, to keep my mouth shut. And to never turn my back on Herbert. I learned, too, not to question Herbert's wisdom, nor his judgment, nor his emotions. At least not in any way that he could perceive any questioning displeasure or censure.

The second time he threatened me, he knocked on my door with an eight-pound sledge hammer. He announced that if I were to join Walter's family up in the parlor, he, Herbert, would destroy the contents of my room, my new twelve-string Framus guitar included. Herbert had an arresting way of choosing his weapons to threaten me with. He had a commanding way of getting my attention and throwing me headlong into the world of irrational danger.

Slipping carefully through and around and between the rubble and the debris of Herbert's emotional outbursts and frightening silences over the first few weeks and months after his first threat, I became something of a friend of his. One safe and soft evening in the warmth and familiarity of his room, he told me his story.

Being the youngest of four boys of a German farm family during the WW II years, Herbert had not been required to actively join the German forces, though the Hitler Youth had been part of his requisite learning. It was early in 1942 and Herbert's brothers, all three of them, were holed up in Stalingrad with the rest of the Wehrmacht, shut down, halted and immobilized around that awful Russian city with its unbearable Russian muskeg, bog, and climate.

"Herbert!" bellowed his father into the courtyard that fall day through his high office window, his voice echoing around the U-shaped courtyard framed by the all-in-one house, barn, and shed arrangement. "*Komm hier*, Herbert!"

Herbert acknowledged his father's call, carefully skirted the perfectly square-sided manure pile in the middle of the courtyard, and hurried up the stairs to the house and his father's office. Hitler youth knew the wisdom of not dawdling when called. A little fearfully, Herbert knocked at the door and stepped into the nearly sacred sanctum of his father's office. The boy stood at attention, more like a soldier reporting for duty than a 14-year-old coming to talk with his father.

"As you know, Herbert, we have not heard from your brothers in some weeks now. It has been reported that things are not going well in Stalingrad. I have obtained permission from our local commandant for you to ride with the supply trains to the

Russian front. I have bought you this new coat, the weather is cold. Do you like the colors? Mother has baked some sweets and prepared some packages for your brothers for you to take to them. You will leave early tomorrow. I trust that a boy of your age, who is old enough to be a soldier in the Fuhrer's army, can find his brothers, give them our gifts, and then report back to me. I think this journey will make a man out of you. I wish you safety. Let me shake your hand."

Herbert's father was nowhere to be seen at 4:30 a.m. the next morning when his mother shook Herbert awake. With a hurried breakfast of dark bread, a little quark, and more words than usual from his mother, Herbert was surprised by the tight but quick hug she gave him. He ran to the train station as directed. In his duffel bag were the packages for his brothers and a bulging bag of bread, cheese, boiled eggs, and even, surprisingly, a precious bon-bon, the latter obviously acquired by a mother's magic in the midst of a luxury-less war.

The train was, naturally, precisely on time and Herbert settled into his seat. Afraid but brave. From Mannheim to Berlin to places in Poland and into Russia itself, sometimes on trucks in long columns, sometimes even on foot with horses and heavy packs, Herbert began to understand some of the adventure, some of the hardships of war.

Often the replacement soldiers and couriers hid in the roadside brush as planes flew overhead, drop-ping bombs and spraying the road with machine-gun fire. Day and night passed for Herbert almost without notice. Some 14 days after leaving his home, Herbert stood on the fringes of Stalingrad, next to the commandant who had granted Herbert's father the permission for Herbert to go along and had tak-en the responsibility to deliver the boy to his broth-ers at the front. The commandant was grim-faced.

Fighting was heavy, from what Herbert could

tell, as batteries of guns and mortars fired away into the city. It seemed even to the young untrained Herbert that the Russian return fire was easily as intense as the German attack, if not more so. For the first time, Herbert realized that the war was really a solemn thing, not only the hype and the pride and the flag waving that was so much a part of the Youth movement. Even yet, Herbert did not know that Germany was losing here, and losing was not a part of Hitler's plan nor of any German training nor thinking. The bedlam caused great delays. It took time for the officer and the communications sergeant on whom Herbert had to depend to locate his brothers and their divisions. When it seemed there was no organization left, and surprise upon surprise, the Russians were pushing the Germans out, Herbert finally found his brothers.

He was not prepared for what he found. He saw all three of them within the space of a few hours, but he talked to none of them. All three of them were dead. Killed in the brutal fighting. Only later would Herbert know that he had arrived just as the Russians were defeating the Germans, and the war was turning. While he did see the broken and mangled, shrapnel-scarred bodies of his three brothers, there was little time left but to seek his own escape. By the time Herbert found his commandant, the Germans were being routed, and he was told that there was no space left on the carriers for a 14-year-old boy on a family visit. The commandant tersely informed Herbert that he would have to find his own way home.

Herbert watched a few straggling trucks loaded with broken soldiers heading on the road south, and he turned toward Mannheim and his beloved Deutschland on foot. Somehow he knew this would be a long journey. He wondered at his father's words: Would this make him a man? By the end of the first day, Herbert knew he would need to be resourceful if he were going to eat, if he were going to live. There seemed few Germans left on this walk, and crazy Russian peasants, some with guns, some with knives, nearly all with some farm tool such as a pitchfork or a hammer, shouted at and threatened anything that was German.

Not only frightened, Herbert was confused by this lack of respect for, and the lack of power of, his German being. Soon he was stealing food out of gardens and slinking around the back kitchens of homes in Russian villages. He hardly knew where south was anymore, he just followed his stomach to eat and his instincts to stay alive. He slept in barns, dug into straw stacks, and balanced himself high up in trees in forests and wood lots, hoping always to be undiscovered by wild-eyed horsemen or toothless and brutish peasant women in a world that was suddenly completely hostile.

Herbert never saw himself in these days, never a mirror did he look into, since he wasn't even in a house for months. It's a good thing he didn't see himself, for the wildness that was appearing in his eyes, the gauntness of his cheeks, the grayness of his skin, and the stoop of his shoulders would have horrified the 14-year-old. He just kept fighting to stay alive, to survive.

Somewhere in Poland after weeks, maybe months, of wandering and starvation, a heavy hand yanked him out of the ditch he was sleeping in, and Herbert was thrown into a decrepit and unlit jail cell. With room for about six men in the cell, the dozen and a half or more of imbeciles and hardened types, both men and women, made for new horrors. A German teenager was an easy and defenseless target in this place. Herbert couldn't recall all that happened in that cell; he just shuddered at its memory. One day a drunken guard forgot to lock the cell. By morning Herbert was out of that hell, and he was running and walking in the mud and the rain, hoping that what was ahead of him was south. Now Herbert began to dream about seeing his mother and father again.

Seeking shelter from the ceaseless drizzle in a huge barn of what must have been a wealthy Polish farmer, Herbert hid for days unnoticed. He stole from the pigs rich morsels of throwaway people food, and the boy, grown old too soon, wondered at times about being of the superior Aryan race. He wondered how long it would be until he was home. He got sick hiding in that barn and Herbert guessed that he had fainted or something and a hired hand must have found him. Vaguely he remembered a bed, and some soup being served him, and then bombs and fire, and again running in the night, in the rain. Beyond that there was a blank space. Time lost. Herbert could remember nothing of some months, maybe even a year.

Back on the road again, Herbert began to notice more and more German being spoken in the villages he was slinking through. He stayed away from soldiers, even those who were German-speaking. He had learned to trust no one; to fear everyone. Nothing seemed to hurt much anymore. He mostly just felt anger. Talking to no one, ever, Herbert spent most of his time muttering and swearing. Cursing everything.

Month after month, even year after year, Herbert worked his way south towards his home, doing odd jobs, working for farmers who often just paid him with food. By now he was in no hurry to get home; he didn't relish the idea of telling his parents that his brothers were dead. It never crossed his mind that they would have known long ago.

Finally Herbert was within 50 kilometers of his home village. He dragged his feet now. It took him a week to walk that distance; more and more he reviewed his childhood and what it had been like before he had left to find his brothers in Stalingrad.

Herbert was now 18 years old. His walk home had taken four years. He was within sight of his home-town Lutheran church steeple by five one afternoon and he looked down on his village from a ridge of higher hills. The village looked so peaceful, so unlike anything in his last four years. The valley hung with more smoke than he remembered as normal, but then so much else had changed, he was no longer surprised at anything.

Herbert decided not to go home yet. He needed one more night. He settled himself against a small hay mound knowing he would get little sleep. He needed to think; he knew tomorrow his life would change again. He wondered what it would be like to have people around; what it would be like to have a family, a home, a place, a belonging. Then he remembered his first task would be to report to his stern father. Somehow he had to find a way to tell the news so that it didn't sound like it was his fault that his brothers had died. Herbert dozed off and on, dreaming that he was crying, running in slow motion, but never able to get away from rid-dled bleeding bodies chasing him with weapons. Somewhere from his own village, a rooster crowed and roused the sleeping teenager. Herbert was now ready to enter his home town by six in the morning.

Herbert stole into town. He met no one in the narrow twisting street, except a few people reaching out their doors for milk containers, and a few hired hands shoveling manure in the courtyards. Herbert entered the street he could have found with his eyes closed. His home would be around the slight curve, six houses from the main corner. He rounded the gentle curve, hoping now not to see anyone and even a little excited at the prospect of seeing his mother. Herbert stopped in his tracks. There was no house, no barn, no shed, no courtyard–just a gaping hole of emptiness, where he remembered it all to be. There was just a mound of ashes–smoldering ashes, gleaming orange when the gentle wind stirred the surface. Wisps of lazy smoke rose from the ash heap and drifted into the morning sky. Herbert stared. He looked around. All the other buildings and yards stood as always, even the geranium boxes in all the house windows were exactly as they had always been. He looked back to his space, expecting, or was it simply hoping, that he had been deluded and it would now be standing as it always had. A green door hanging a little crooked in an old stone frame. But there was no green door—there was no stone frame—just devastation. It must have been a massive fire, for nothing, not a brick nor a stone, was standing in the rubble. Everything was black.

Herbert heard a step behind him. Herr Schnabele, a neighbor, came out of his house and stepped toward Herbert. He started to greet the young stranger when a dark look of recognition clouded over his face. "Herbert? Are you Herbert?"

"Yes, what...?"

"Oh, Herbert, your parents. Your house. It burned yesterday and your parents, they both were in the fire."

Herbert fell to the street, screaming. The neighbors gathered from up and down the village. On his face in the road, Herbert pounded the cobblestone with his fists and screamed. And cursed. He cursed as if he were entering hell itself.

I don't know where Herbert is anymore. Somebody came in a car and took him away from Walter's place one day some months after he told me his story. I know his madness was a way to survive. I don't blame him for having wanted to spear a cheeky kid who thought life was made up of simple decisions. I know that his anger was a mechanism to keep out all the pain that lived in his soul. I also know that sometimes the ones who die in war are luckier than those who don't. At least their death stops hurting.

Loss, death, despair, madness and survival, the hell of war, and even the hell of life is what the story of Herbert is about.

Herbert being sent to find his brothers reminds us of another brother, Joseph, being sent to find his brothers a long time ago. The Bible writer paints the story of Joseph early in the record, and in and around the most-favored son and most-hated brother scenario, we get an answer to Cain's question, "Am I my brother's keeper?" Joseph answers it with touches and tears of forgiveness, bags of grain, a new home, and a new life for his family. Rather a surprising response to the death talk and the slave-selling stuff Joseph must have remembered about his brothers from the last time he was with them. What's happened to the "eye for an eye" treatment we so often think the Old Testament is rife with?

One can so clearly see the Author, the Redeemer standing behind the magnificently told Joseph story. He who would have all brothers hold back their hand from killing their siblings, he who would have all brothers returning love for hate, kept his eye, I believe, on the frightened and devastated Herbert throughout his sojourn. The God who resides above us is often said to be cold-hearted in holding back his hand when he could so easily tweak to death with his celestial finger, in a millisecond, those who abuse children, those who trample the small and the helpless, those who exploit all who can be exploited, and those who start wars. But God is a great independence Giver. It is precisely because he is not cruel that he lets humankind experience the consequences for its own sin and nonsense. Then and often only then does his Spirit swoop down as a Redeemer and make good to come from evil. So a son lost and nearly killed and sold into slavery becomes a savior; a dynamite charge set to blow up a well to deprive an Arab farmer of water in the aftermath of another Arab-Israeli war, opens a better well; and a teenager dying of leukemia counsels and comforts dozens of children dying, too, from the horror of cancer, and makes their deaths easier before she is gone.

21

God so often turns the stifling stuff of a hellish life into the surprising substance of heaven. Herbert, bereft of family, emotionally immobilized, thrown back and forth between raging and periods of precarious tranquillity, is given seasons of madness to hide in, when the horror plagues him too much, when the memories are too unbearable.

When I knew Herbert, he had been given a gentle family to live with and work for. A family who treated him with a dignity and kindness, a graciousness and forgiveness and longsuffering that he hadn't even known in his childhood days before the war when he was just a little boy growing up with his brothers in a small German village.

The God standing back of the Herbert story is not an uninvolved God, never an uncaring God. He is a God who is watching and waiting to turn night into day, crying into laughter, death into life. There is no horror we can endure or imagine, there is no sin we can commit, that is beyond the scope of our Creator and Savior God to remake into something whole and beautiful. God watching over Herbert, weeping for him as he stumbles through life, will not rewrite human history like a 1984 Big Brother writer who wants to reconstruct life in denial; he is a God who waits for the right moment to shower his lovingkindness and renewal on Herbert and make him whole. Of the many things God is, one is that he is a reclaimer of that which is good in the human soul and experience. In God's hand, loss can become foundness, survival can become thriving, despair can become hope, and an earthly hell can be redeemed into paradise.

Herbert, wherever he might be today, I am sure, still limps and falls emotionally through life, but the God of Abraham, Isaac and Jacob waits for Herbert to reach out, cry out, and even scream out for new life, for wholeness, for peace, in spite of all pain.

Walter

I worked for Walter. He was only 30 and I was 20, but that 10-year span between 20 and 30 is like 25 sometimes.

The deal was that I would work for six months. I would get two weeks of holidays and the equivalent of $15 per month, all necessities provided. I worked hard–cleaning the barns, harvesting sugar beets, checking the hen barns every morning–though I drove the tractor into a drainage ditch and bent the frame on his new Opel by dropping a wheel off the too-narrow road when I gave too much space to an oncoming car. But Walter took all the accidents in stride.

After the first three or four weeks, Walter suggested that I take a week off, though I was not to count it as holidays. Before I left in the fog the next morning, backpack high on my back, sleeping bag tightly rolled up and stuck up under the frame, Walter pressed $30 into my hand, double what it was agreed he would pay me per month.

When I walked back up the winding lane into the yard a week later, getting the stenchy eye-burning whiff of the chicken manure from the barn ventilation stacks, I had resolved that I would repay this kind man with extra work.

The next morning I was up a half hour earlier than our agreed starting time, and I started to look for ways to do the extra work. By the end of the second month Walter remarked that I was working beyond the call of duty. This time he rolled $45 into my hand and announced at the breakfast table that I would be given the next week off, and he added that this, too, was not part of my holidays. This was simply bonus time.

"Go and see our Europe," he laughed, "and come back and tell us of your adventures, of our continent. We have really seen very little of it, not so, Heinz?" he nodded to one of the hired men, who had not ever been further than 80 kilometers from his little home village where he lived in the house in which he had been born.

I walked out to the road a second time, smiling at my 'good luck', amazed at the graciousness of this simple but profound man who knew what it meant to empower and bless and bring out the best in me.

I scanned the rolling hills in both directions along the narrow German road, watching to see from which direction the first car would come, because its direction of travel would decide which way my journey would take this day. I thought of what I would say to Walter when my time with him was finished.

Four months later, I stood outside the door of the house on the cobblestone pavement. My bags were packed, and a car had come to take me to another place, another adventure. Another young man was coming to replace me. While Walter laughed easily, I think he wondered at my reckless-ness in hugging him and telling him, "Walter, I have worked for you for six months. You have been gen-erous beyond my wildest dreams in time off and pay given. I feel that after six months, I am eight months behind in what I owe you. You remind me of Someone."

The generosity of God, the graciousness of God is nearly beyond the descriptors that we word-play-ers can find. I don't "meet God halfway." It's like I inch a centimeter toward him; and he gallops a mile to touch me. It's not so much, "When I go out seek-ing Thee, I find Thee seeking me," as it is me looking out the window thinking about his possible coming, and he has already driven up the lane.

Sometimes I see myself living my life in a great coat that I have tightly wrapped around myself to protect me from others, from exposure, from outside facts that would alter my views. On those few occasions that I have the courage, or is it the fear, to open up to God, I open the great coat just a little, and he floods my body, my being, my soul and spirit with his warmth, with his power, with himself. And I am amazed at him, even as I pull the coat tightly around myself again, still thinking that I must do it myself, like a two-year-old standing in her high chair with no way to get out, but insisting on being able to do so.

God gives himself to us, to his creation beyond our dreams and imaginings. He is generous; he is gracious. He is the ultimate gift giver. We can never pay him back for what he has given us in himself, in his Son, in his Spirit, and as we hand back to him our crumbs, he just pours more on us. He is more than we can imagine. He is Walter, but a million times more, and then another million times.

Onkel Heinrich

Onkel Heinrich, as I was asked to address him, was the patriarch of a traditional Swabish German family in south central Germany. Having fathered and raised a dozen children, managed a successful farming operation, and grown up in an austere and severe family system himself, Onkel Heinrich seldom allowed his children to speak to him unless he had spoken to them first, even as adults. Onkel Heinrich chose whether there would be conversation between him and anyone else, totally on his own whim. I was astounded to watch him at meal time being meticulously served by his faithful wife and daughters. He ate what he wanted, and he burped when he was finished as if he were a king—and he was.

I think that Onkel Heinrich was amused by me. I think he was amused by my ignorance of the mores of his society and by my naive obliviousness to breaking the social rules of his culture, home, and family. Nevertheless, he seemed to take a liking to me and often invited me on many evenings to his private study to eat sweet cookies, drink dry white wine, and talk about the American space program, the Church in America, the War, and what would possess my parents to let me leave home and come to work in Germany.

I found out soon enough that some of Onkel Heinrich's children, not so much older than I, were resentful of my time and conversations, and even a kind of friendship, with their dad. They had never experienced any affection nor even shared any meaningful conversation with him.

Onkel Heinrich employed a number of people on his farm: two hired men and a half-dozen women to gather the eggs, clean the barns, and harvest the sugar beets if the rains had come early and the fields were too sodden to harvest the beets with machinery. By observation, I soon noticed that though Onkel Heinrich seemed to like his workers, he never said "Please!" nor "Thank you!" to them. I think he thought that as the boss it was simply not necessary to engage in such niceties. How could it ever be assumed that they were doing him a favor, or had extended him a kindness? They were doing their job, for which they would be paid. I noticed just as quickly, though, that when he wished me to do something, he asked me, politely, and afterwards thanked me. I wondered about this for a number of months.

When the day came for me to move to another job in another part of Europe, Onkel Heinrich stood in the knot of people who were saying goodbye as I was leaving.

Onkel Heinrich stood smiling, and I felt relatively sure he felt some affection for me and some sadness that I was leaving. I shook hands around the circle, ending with Onkel Heinrich. "Bless you, young man," he said.

"May I ask you a question before I go, Onkel Heinrich?" I queried.

"Well, yes!" he answered.

"Why have you always said 'Please' and 'Thank You' to me, when you never did to the rest of the workers here?"

"Oh, that's not so difficult," he laughed, his face wrinkling around his eyes. "I could tell early on that you were not constituted in a way that would allow you to function without 'Pleases!' and 'Thank yous!' You simply couldn't take it. I did it for you!"

How does God talk to us? Are we treated like minor cousins? Colleagues? Helpless children? Pitiful addicts? Biblical scholars? Motivational speakers? Peasants? Educated servants? Does he take into account how he has made us with our weaknesses, with our strengths?

I don't know how often I have stood before God and said, "Well, I blew it again." But never have I had the sense that he sighs, and then forgives me ever so reluctantly with a mutter about his own good nature. I have never been aware of even a slight edge of annoyance in his voice, nor even a tiny wince of impatience in his eyes. God does not patronize me, humor me, nor toy with me. He talks to me straight out, Spirit to spirit, when I give him my ear, my heart and my spirit, and in that he touches me with so much dignity, I am left with nothing but wide-eyed awe at his being, his kindness, his warmth, his understanding, his ability to make me feel so good about life, about Life.

I saw in Onkel Heinrich strength in leadership, and strength in his fatherhood, and I saw in him glimpses of the strength of God. God breathes an ultimate strength and honest gentleness that empowers me, that holds me up, that gives me the dignity to know I am so loved I can hardly speak, I can only wonder and be warmed. God, our God, sends smiles upon us and draws us into his presence, closer to himself. He is my dignity-giver; he is my Maker. Everyday!

Onkel
Heinrich

The Domine

My experience with elderly church leaders was one-dimensional. Their voices took on the tone of a sepulchre in the pulpit, and when they came to our home for what we children learned to dread as "the housevisits," we were unable to see them as relevant or real. I can remember those old preachers: bearded and Bibled with few smiles and no laughs. Life for these men of the ordained but volunteer cloth was a serious business. Self-indulgence, self-gratification, and any pleasure, it seemed to me, would never be known to these men, except to shout against. The ministers I remember could have given the proverbial Presbyterian lessons on longfacedness, I think, and it never crossed my mind that someday I would be one of them. Either God has an outrageous sense of humor, or he's cruel.

When I was finally teen-ager old enough to be able to choose talking to an Elder or running the other way, I chose not to be available. And I wasn't for years.

I signed up for a Cultural Exchange Program to Europe when I was 19. We gathered in Holland since it was the Dutch contingent's turn of the host organization to orient, brief, and debrief the North Americans before and after their year in Europe. The year passed for me in agony and ecstasy before we spent the final week of the yearlong exchange in a North Sea Conference and Retreat Center. Transformed and reoriented North Americans from conservative and fundamentalist Christian homes brought European mores, German boyfriends, and Dutch girlfriends to the one-week debriefing before the journey home. The group was hardly the same

people who had come fresh-faced from America a
year earlier. Oh, the faces were the same, but the
innocence was gone, and the many and varied experiences had piled up, wised up, and guilted up the
group.

We sat at a long bar late at night. It was the last
night before early morning departure for North
America. I sat at the elbow of a Dutch church leader—the Domine—a bishop. We had seen him skin-
ny-dipping in the fluorescent North Sea amongst
the mixed crowd earlier in the evening. His behavior had gasped us more than the pungent salty air
on the strong ocean wind. On his other elbow a
young Canadian, quiet and always shy in a crowd,
sat with his Dutch girlfriend. The two young lovers
hardly talked. This was their last evening together
before he would go home to the Alberta hills, and
she would resume her level Dutch existence without
her Canadian boyfriend. The Domine heard the
sadness in their infrequent voices, the regret of their
impending separation in their silence. And besides,
how do you say good-bye for 12 hours?

"David," he finally said, "do you two want my
room to spend the last night together?"

Overhearing him, my mind flashed back to my
housevisiting "bishops." They would never have!
There must be a middle ground on this stuff, I
thought. I think the Domine noticed my shock and
he smiled, just a little patronizingly.

❖ ❖ ❖

What's morality? What responsibility does an elder
brother have for the morality of the younger?
Does a "stumbling block" assume full responsibility for
the decisions of the stumblee? Is there a difference
between being permissive and being tolerant? Are we
cursed to live on one continent too indulgently, on
another too puritanically; one generation too stiffly,
the next too loosely? Where do we draw the lines?

Do we have to draw the lines?

God, the Giver of all good things, desires all the best we can imagine. Sometimes, therefore, he suggests we not cut corners, we wait a little on some things so as not to cheapen a good thing. As a result, the world wails away at God as if he were a fun spoiler, a party wrecker. He isn't. To wait on God, to do the stuff, whatever the stuff, in his timing leaves us smiling in paradise. It's hard to believe, sometimes, that God wants us to have fun when I reflect on the way an unsmiling and severe church has so long presented him. I wished I'd known earlier what God has communicated about himself in his letter. He is about joy; he is about ecstasy; he is about delight; he is about jubilation; he is about elation. We should let no one else's judgment, no one else's weakness take away our eyes to see him as he is. We can look for him ourselves through the pages of our own life, through the glasses we own. Look for yourself. He is worth it; your searching journey is worth it.

The Sisters of Mercy

Thomashof is a German retreat center and guest house for retirees perched high up on a hill above Karlsruhe, Germany. I worked at Thomashof for six months and enjoyed, immensely, the privilege of being the first male volunteer to ever work in the almost entirely female domain of Thomashof - a female domain that collectively agreed that almost any work in this place should not be delegated to a man. So I lounged most of the time, washed the car once a week, whether it needed it or not, and picked up and dropped off people at the train station. Generally, I spent my time teasing and attempting to charm the mostly elderly women of the place, most of whom were deaconesses—Mennonite women who had chosen a celibate and service-centered life complete with identifying black and white habits.

Sister Liesel, though not the Mother Superior at the time, was the leader of the group and was hardly ever amused by me. One day she took me aside and asked: "Are you a Christian?"

"Why do you ask?" I answered, grinning.

"Because some of us have grave doubts. You are too happy."

Another of the sisters, Sister Sarah, should have saved herself for the movie Sister Act. She was hilarious in her antics, and her sparkly eyes flashing below her white starched hat could light up a room. She protected me, often, when the serious-sided ones wanted to do me in for some prank, or for having caused someone to laugh.

One Saturday morning while I was sweeping our half of the busy highway that wound its way past Thomashof, Sister Sarah came around to chat with me. I told her that I was hitchhiking to town as soon as I was finished sweeping the street. I noted to her that I would soon be ready to go since the street was already clean and needed to be swept again simply because this was Saturday, and this was Germany.

Sarah sat down on the step and waited for me to finish, her chin in her hands, looking a lot like a little girl in pigtails in an Americana calendar. Putting away my broom and accompanying sweeping tools, I went back to the road and held out my hand to catch a ride into Karlsruhe.

"I've always wondered how people do this," Sarah laughed. "Show me how to hold my hand." She pulled her hand out of the wide sleeve of her black habit and hitched back her little white hat a bit, looking a little rakish for a nun. I explained to her the fine art of hitchhiking, explaining that how you hold your hand is quite different in Germany than it is in Canada, and that we would need to be culturally sensitive if we wished to get a ride.

Sarah grinned and struck up a practice pose with one foot on the curb and one foot on the road waiting for a car to come along. I began to wonder whether I was going to be getting a seventyish nun to spend the day with me in the city.

A car came speeding around the corner. When the driver saw the sister, all black and white, with her hand pointing at the ground where he was supposed to stop his car, I think he slammed on his brakes more out of curiosity and shock than out of a compulsion to give someone a ride. Naturally, he drove too far, but quickly recovered, punched his car into reverse gear, and backed crazily up to us where Sarah stood waiting for him. I think I stood open-mouthed. As soon as the car was opposite her, Sarah yanked open the passenger door and addressed the young German motorist, "I wouldn't ride with you, but my young friend would. Please take him to Karlsruhe." And she motioned to me to get in. I obeyed. Before I closed the car door, Sister Sarah cautioned me against telling Sister Liesel. "She wouldn't understand any of this, nor have any of the fun that we had doing this," she said, and she waved us away, slapping the trunk as the car moved forward. I heard her delightful and infectious cackle of a laugh as we sped off, a laugh that so often annoyed her silent sisters, but brought the life of smiles to many people at Thomashof.

Some who follow Jesus, some who are "seeking hard after God" have thought that we must live with furrowed brows, heavy with the gravity of being in God's presence. Not all of God's human creations, however, are gifted with a melancholy personality. How, then, must the rest of us live?

I know that followers of Jesus have suffered for their faith throughout the ages, and we are told that more have died for their Christian faith in this century than in all previous centuries of the past two thousand years combined. All of that notwithstanding, I cannot find a scriptural call to dourness, nor can I discern a Jesus call to despondency in the articulation of his gospel, the Good News. In bringing us salvation, Jesus has clearly brought us joy–joy that can be and routinely is enjoyed by his filled followers even in the midst of oppression, tragedy, hunger, war and death. Jesus is not about happiness, something that happens to us; he is about joy, something that includes happiness, but is far greater and far deeper, and lives in spite of all the gulags that life can dish out to us.

Jesus is the joy-giver. If there is no bounce in our step, no sparkle in our eye that anyone can ever notice, it may well be true that Jesus and his Spirit have really not found a home in our hearts, nor has his friendly Spirit actually been able to invade us.

To know Jesus is to know God; to know God is to know joy. There is no other way. There is little else to say.

Minding the Mystery

The Tourist

To be a unilingual Anglophone in Paris doesn't give one the feeling of being much loved by the crowds of chic dressers and easy kissers within sight of the Arc de Triomphe. But I wandered around Paris in my shabby blue jeans and old runners anyway, feeling like I owned the place at least as much as any tourist I had seen. Within a few days of coming to Paris and not being able to find anyone who would speak English to me, I settled down to learn the language. "*Bonjour! Merci! Pardon! Comment ca va?*" soon tripped off my tongue like a Quebecer, but my language skills still didn't seem to make me any friends on the Champs Elysees.

My primary mode of transportation around Paris was walking; my secondary mode was riding the subway train, the Metro. Rush hour was the best time to ride the rubber-tired Metro to watch the Parisians and to be with them.

One Friday evening, I pushed my way to board a packed train headed for the Latin Quarter. Sardined in between Parisians of all shapes and sizes, I fell to drinking in the human sights and waited for something to happen, a story to unfold. As the train started forward, the force of acceleration moved the mass of us standing toward the rear of the train. As we all fought to keep our feet planted, we all leaned in the same direction. When the train stopped the scene reversed itself as we now all leaned as a mass towards the front of the train. All of us tried to keep our balance without becoming too familiar with all the bodies pressed in around us. Every time the train started and stopped its journey across the basement of this famous city, I, unused to the move-

ment, had to catch my balance with a quick movement and repositioning of my feet. At one stop I
stepped on the patented leather shoe of the superbly
coifed and impeccably dressed young man next to
me.

"Oh, *merci!*" I muttered, putting what I hoped
was a tone of apology to my French. My victim just
scowled and looked the other way. At the next stop,
I again could not hold my balance and trampled the
poor young Parisian's shiny toes again.

"*Merci!*" I repeated, louder this time in case he
hadn't heard me the first time. He scowled again,
and I noted the look on his face which says that
foreigners are of a lesser intelligence and should just
stay home. But he said nothing.

At the next stop, the train stopped even more
suddenly than before, and this time, I think I
crunched the poor man's toes nearly flat as I fought
to keep from falling down.

"*Merci!*" I almost shouted, and I am sure that
this time he heard me. Finally, I thought, I'll get
some acknowledgment for my apologies. But the
young man, noting, I guess, my sincerity, seemed
thunderstruck. His face was dark with rage, and seeing his outrage, it suddenly dawned on me what I
had been saying. I wasn't apologizing to the urban
sophisticate; I was thanking him for the privilege of
trouncing him every time the train stopped. I
pushed to the door and got out at the next stop. We
weren't even half way to the Latin Quarter yet. I
didn't care.

God doesn't do dumb things; he doesn't embarrass
himself. But he must have a sense of humor. How
else would he be able to explain the creation of some
of his creations. Neither does he, however, treat those
of us in our stupid moments with disdain. He always
treats us with dignity, allowing us to make the choices

we are determined to make and yet, mercifully, some-times lets us off the hook from having to suffer the consequences for our own actions. While God loves us enough to let us learn our own lessons, there are times his love lets us skip the penalty box completely, such as when he sent his son Jesus to die for all the dumb stuff we all do as naturally as breathing. When I realize that God doesn't scowl at my stupidity, I can stay on the train of his salvation and go free, no shame, no blame. God is my Savior, my unconditional love Sav-ior, who asks only that I stay with him and not get off and run, too afraid to face him and too mortified to accept his grace.

God is wise; God does not get unhinged. God will let me run to my lemming death if I want to, but what makes the Creator smile is when you and I reach up and take his hand and let him pour his grace and goodness upon us, all over and forever.

Abdullah

We drove through the stark wilderness between Jerusalem and Jericho hoping to find Abdullah. Abdullah is a Bedouin Sheik, the head of a mid-sized clan of Bedouin which still clings to its traditionally primitive lifestyle, despite new Jeep Wagoneers outside their tents and TV antennae mounted on their ridge poles.

We drove past a few clusters of camel-hide tents surrounded by tractors and gaggles of kids and dogs, before Mosche, our driver and guide, stopped the car. While we stayed behind, Mosche walked up through the barren scree-like sand and rocks toward a large tent huddled up against a huge rock. A Bedouin woman, in a black dress with a brightly embroidered bib, moved slowly down the hill toward Mosche. As they met, Mosche turned his back to the woman and spoke to her his shoulder, being careful not to make any eye contact with her. Their conversation was brief, with the woman gesturing toward the hilly horizon, obviously telling Mosche that Abdullah was in one of the wadis in the area, or out visiting some of his clansmen somewhere east of us in the wilderness. Mosche came back to the car.

"Now we just wait," he said. "Now that one of Abdullah's people knows we're here, he will now know too."

"How?" we asked.

"These remarkable people have a mysterious and mystical way of communicating with one another that we modern folk will never know," he said, "and I can predict that Abdullah will be here soon. We can only wait."

We settled into the soft seats of the car as
Mosche told us stories of the Bedouin. How they
know when someone has walked across their land at
night. How they can be assembled and ready with a
feast for a distinguished traveler as he arrives, even
though he had never notified them that he was
coming.

"There he is!" shouted Mosche. And there he
was. A lone man, wrapped in flowing robes of
white and brown, head wrapped in the traditional
kaffiyeh, coming toward us across the desert. Looking like an apparition of Lawrence of Arabia, Abdullah silenced us with his charisma and his presence
across the dust between us. Mosche sprang out of
the car, motioning us to remain behind. We
watched as Bedouin royalty and Israeli scholar and
soldier met and embraced, warmly, kissing on one
cheek, then the other, and back to the first. The
body language told us these men held each other in
high regard. Mosche paid his proper respects and
then brought Abdullah back to us. We stood out of
the car and shook hands, awed, and greatly taken by
this man who exuded a presence that somehow
embarrassed our own ordinariness.

Mosche inquired as to Abdullah's health and his
sons. Was Allah providing? Were his sons well?
Were the animals well supplied with ample pastures
this year?

His handsome leathery brown and wind-blown
face framed by his white linen kaffiyeh, its ends
blowing in the desert breeze, the hospitable Abdullah invited us to his private tent some miles away.
He rode with us in the Jeep and remained quiet as
Mosche briefed us in English as to the protocol
when we would arrive at Abdullah's tent.

As we later followed Abdullah and Mosche up
the wadi to his tent, we were met by children obviously respectful and fond of this man. Dogs of
questionable character barked and growled at us.

Nearing a large tent, Mosche motioned us to stop. Abdullah indicated what must have been his wishes to some women busy in a tent. Mosche moved around to tell us more of the Bedouin ways and stood facing in such a way that we would not be looking over his shoulder at the women now busy making tea, scolding children, and shooing baby lambs and goats out of their way.

Abdullah

Mosche informed us that the two women busy in the main tent were both Abdullah's wives. We were quick to note a forty-something woman, clearly in charge, working with a mid-twenty-year-old woman, obviously pregnant.

Abdullah motioned for us to be seated in the second tent, which had little but a rug on the floor, in contrast to the primary tent that contained some furniture, cooking facilities, and sleeping mats. Through Mosche, he explained to us that though this was a strictly men's tent, the young western women with us were welcome to join the men for tea in this tent since it seemed to him western women were used to being treated as men.

Abdullah's wives brought the tea to the corner of the tent while he poured the piping hot peppermint and black tea mixture into small handle-less white cups. Since there were too few cups for the size of our party, Abdullah waited for those first served to finish their tea before he rinsed out the empty cups with hot water and quickly served those waiting from the same cups.

When we had all drunk, Abdullah sat with Mosche on the rug, and Mosche invited Abdullah to speak with us and invited us to be ready to ask questions. Abdullah briefly outlined his personal history and the size and range of his property and holdings. As we asked questions, Abdullah seemed to become uneasy. Mosche remarked to us in English that we westerners laugh too easily as answers to our questions are translated back to us;

Abdullah was feeling that we were laughing at him. We should continue to be interested as he spoke, but we should not laugh any more, cautioned Mosche..

After some time, Mosche indicated we should leave. We stood up, shook hands with Abdullah, thanking him through Mosche for his hospitality, and returned to our car.

Mosche explained to us on the way back to Jerusalem that one of Abdullah's nephews had been killed by a neighboring Bedouin some time ago. Now one of the nephew's relatives was obligated to avenge the death. The murderer's family, in the meantime, had bought thirty revenge-free days from Abdullah and his clan with the gift of a new Chevrolet. Today, however, was the twenty-ninth day of the peace pact, Mosche told us, and Abdullah was somewhat distracted, deeply concerned as to what might happen next between his clan and the neighboring clan come the end of the thirtieth day, tomorrow.

I never saw Abdullah again, nor did we ever hear if the conflict between Abdullah and his neighbors was peacefully resolved. I shall never forget, however, the gravity, the depth, and the personal power that exuded from this man. Wisdom and strength seemed to sit on him, and in remembering him, I will always feel he knew a lot more about us than we could ever know about him.

If a person can wordlessly and without show project power and even a sense of majesty, how much more can God the Creator, of whom Abdullah is just a small image, emanate power and majesty. Often in the Bible we read descriptions of worshippers on their faces before God. We individualistic, God-unto-ourselves westerners don't go down on our faces very much. We will have to be pretty awed to fall on our faces out of choice when we stand before the forever God and give account for the state of our souls.

Abdullah was a practicing Muslim, with all the desert manifestations of the Islamic faith, but it was easy for me to see that he was made in the image of God. Thinking of the Being who created Abdullah, I look forward with anticipation and fear to standing and lying before our God in all awareness.

I know, too, that we cynical westerners find it difficult to believe that these primitive people of the desert can communicate with each other in nonverbal, non-technical without-a-cell-phone ways, but even in this, Abdullah worked with a little part of God in him by using the ability to connect with people close to him by way of thought transfer. God knows what we think, he knows what we know, he knows what we need. God is in communication with us and we with him in ways beyond our understanding. I do hope and pray, and plan to stand and lie in wonder before him some day. And certainly it is true that he knows far more of me than I of him. The best I can pray for is to be reverently agnostic about him.

Ibrahim

Ibrahim sits on the low wall outside the Jaffa Gate in Old Jerusalem, waiting. Waiting for someone to need his strong back and his determined strength to carry and move things for them. Ibrahim is a porter. One of many porters who wait for hourly and daily jobs about the city of Jerusalem in exchange for the money they need to keep themselves and their loved ones fed.

Ibrahim carried things whichever way he could, sometimes on his back, and sometimes rigged into a hemp and sack-like frame and harness to keep the objects attached to himself. We had seen Ibrahim walking down Jaffa Street with a refrigerator on his back, so bent over that the door of the fridge was parallel to the sidewalk. We had seen Ibrahim carrying huge wicker baskets on his back filled with long loaves of bread or running over with grapes. We had seen Ibrahim sitting and talking with his younger porter colleagues; Ibrahim was no longer a young man.

We heard the story one day of how, one Saturday, Ibrahim was carrying a wicker basket full of wood down one of the narrow streets of East Jerusalem. Coming up the long steps toward the outer edges of the city, Ibrahim was suddenly face to face with an avid Sabbath keeper. The devout one spit in Ibrahim's face and cursed him for desecrating the sacred land with his unnecessary work on the Sabbath. Ibrahim had wiped the spittle from his face and answered his attacker with the words: "Because of Jesus, I refuse to spit back in your face. Because of Jesus, I refuse to hate you for what you have just done to me. Because of Jesus, I forgive you your actions, and I ask you to forgive me for having offended you."

The power and the poise of Jesus still walks the streets of Jerusalem some two thousand years later.

"The Sabbath was made for man, not man for the Sabbath" stands out as one of Christ's richest phrases among all of his wonderfully pithy and powerful statements. Christ's teachings are rife with the message that man has dignity–incredible, inviolate dignity. One of the remarkable devices that the Creator established to protect the dignity of humankind was the Sabbath–that break day in life that gives rhythm and height and depth to existence. God knows that boredom and sameness in life ekes the essence out of the living, so he instituted the Sabbath, and ordered its observance to lend dignity to our existence.

If, then, the Sabbath is really a device to ensure our dignity, what might we say has happened that people think they can spit in someone's face for not observing it—where has the awareness of the dignity of the human gone? Or did the Sabbath Keeper believe that such a spitting as he rendered Ibrahim might ensure ongoing dignity for others? He might have. But I doubt that God would want dignity trampled in order that a mechanism be saved; I doubt that God, the Creator of relationships, who sent his son to die that we might have an unfettered relationship with him, wanted an institutionalized day to be sacred above a human being. People, not a specific day of the week, are made in God's image. It doesn't matter even if it is the best day of the week; it is not more important than a person.

Clearly, God is dignity infuser and dignity keeper. He made us, and he saw us, even in our fallenness, so worthwhile, he reckoned us worth dying for. We are chosen, holy, royal, a people; imagine, if God's word calls us so much, what he must be, since we are only but chips off the Divine Block. If God says to us, "You're worth it!" who are we to say we're not! God is the ultimate worth-giver, the dignity stroker, the commissioner of honor upon us. He makes me feel so good when I am aware that I am in his presence.

Defying Death

The Paint Brothers

Finally at 18 the call of the city to a country kid became too loud. I turned toward the bright lights and went looking for work. I could drive a tractor and handle a truck loaded with grain, but I wasn't sure what I could do in the city. I remembered that my brother had taken this same journey some 10 years earlier, so I walked in his steps wherever I could. I remembered that he had worked at Filip's Paints. I caught a N. Main bus up to the corner of Main and Logan and stepped off. Nothing on a southern Manitoba farm prepares a kid for the culture of Main and Logan, and I hurried up towards King Street away from the needy and unruly street people shouting at me for a dime. I resisted the weak Sunday school Samaritan urge to stop and help the drunk passed-out on the sidewalk that all the street priests just stepped around. Nobody else seemed to care or even notice a man who I thought might even be dead.

It didn't take me long to find the paint factory with the retail and wholesale outlet up front. I told the clerk in one sentence that my brother had worked here some years ago, and that I was looking for a job. After a quickly arranged on-the-spot interview, I was hired for my first real job. "Sixty-four dollars a week, in cash. Payday's every Friday, and you work every second Saturday 'til noon," said Eddie, the store manager, and he smiled. Now I became frightened in the paint store more than I had been uneasy on Logan and Main not a half hour earlier. Responsibility and growing up can be discomforting.

I worked in the retail store. Selling paint. Talking paint. Mixing paint. Spilling paint. I met painters and would-be painters. I met people with paint in their hair, paint in their veins, and paint on their brains. And every Friday I got a little brown envelope with three twenties, three ones, and four quarters in it. One Friday I said I had been shortchanged a dollar. I didn't notice the crisp new one dollar bill stuck to the side of the envelope. The bookkeeper undertook a forensic investigation to find the dollar, yelling at every one in the office, including the bosses, whose main interest in life seemed to be centered on the State of Israel, until I sheepishly announced I had just found the dollar in my envelope. An hour after the huge investigation had been launched, the bookkeeper now yelled at me. She told me I was lucky they weren't going to fire me. I began to wish they would so that I could disappear.

One midsummer day at noon, the foreman announced in the lunchroom that he would need someone to stay late, to work overtime. A huge paint order had come in. I cautiously said I could stay, as the foreman glowered at the rest of the staff, all of them suddenly studying paint specks on the floor.

"Check in with George in the plant when you're done in the store at five," growled the foreman. "He's stayin' to make a batch of red paint for the order that just came in for Versatile. Don't think it's going to be easy. George is our regular white-paint maker and his brother, Harry, is our red-paint maker. Harry's sick. George said he'd make the red paint if he had tuh! Check in with George as soon as you're off. He'll take you for supper to the New Nanking before you start work. Filip's paying!"

I had never eaten Won Ton soup before. It turned my stomach; made me feel woozy. Having someone else pay for it, however, made me feel better, and I even kept the fortune cookie down that had said, *Things will get better!* After George chewed three toothpicks, we walked the evening Logan

Avenue back to the plant and went to work.

Somewhere on that walk from the New Nanking Restaurant back to Filip's Paint something happened to George. He started cursing. When he unlocked the plant door and slid the huge door sideways to open it up, he kicked a 5 gallon pail over, and picking up a broken spade handle, he punctured a 50 pound bag of brilliant red powder pigment like a sealer off the Newfoundland coast. The powder whooshed out the broken bag and spread around our feet like flowing blood. George was having a tantrum. I stayed back far enough to not get caught in this one man electrical storm but close enough to hear his orders. After all, without George telling me I would have no idea what to do.

George barked at me to carry this bag, pour that chemical, and move that far pallet until I began to feel like I was trapped too close to a fire that could explode in any direction at any moment.

"Red paint! Flippin' red paint!" he fumed. "I don't know why I have to make this stuff. Seventeen years of white paint and what do I get?" And then his anger turned into sarcasm. "Stay late, George, and make red paint! Please, George. Harry's sick and you're the only one that can do it. Please, George. Where in the hay did these guys learn 'Please!' I've never heard that before. And you can better well guess there'll be no thanks in the morning either!"

I felt responsible to control the outraged paint maker, so I tested a question,

"Have you really been making white paint for 17 years?"

"Yes." he shouted. "What do you think?"

"Just white? Never red?" I asked, incredulously.

"Never!" he roared. "I hate red! I wouldn't be caught dead making red!"

"You'd think," I volunteered, being clearly as stupid as I had ever been in my entire 18 years, "that making red paint after just making white paint for

17 years, uh, would be a nice change."

They say that it feels good to sit down in a good chair after a hard day of physical work and just watch the sun go down. That night I sat down long after I had managed to slip out of Filip's Paint still shaking but happy that I had escaped so narrowly becoming one of the substances that George used to make the 250 gallon batch of red paint that day. I have often thought I must have had the same value to George as an airborne five gallon pail or an impaled bag of rosy pigment around the paint plant for the rest of the shift. I wondered, too, what he might have told the foreman about how much of a help I had been.

I don't know if George got to get back to peacefully making white paint for the rest of his life or not; I, on the other hand, haven't made any red or white paint myself since that day. The routine of my life is too set; I wouldn't like to upset my regular routine to make paint with all the other stuff I'm in the habit of making every day.

In a world that is changing in ways faster than we can comprehend at speeds beyond what we can imagine, it is reassuring to know that God is unchanging. God is the same, "Yesterday, today and forever!" in nature, but I get the sense that God loves change. Change is what God's Son came to give us. To know forgiveness, to live forgiveness, is to mellow, is to be transformed towards a calmness of spirit that doesn't come naturally to most of us. Routines lie to us that we can expect life to proceed without bumps, without surprises. The best things in my life are the changes, the surprises, the things that happened to me, the people that happened to me, who appeared without me manipulating or inventing their existence in my days.

God is, though, by far the biggest surprise. That he so much puts up with my weakness' and my lack of discipline can only mean that God is completely un-hung up. He rolls with the punches so to speak, his love for me overriding the annoyance and impatience he would feel if he were me, or like me. God is not like me; I am like him, but in minute ways that I pray are increasing. I celebrate his changing in me through his unchanging love for me.

The Voice In the Crowd

It was October 1972 and the American military machine had announced that it was going to test an underground nuclear device in the Amchita Islands in the Alaskan Panhandle. The anti-American press whipped the Canadian public into a frenzy that the fallout from the test would drift across Canada with the prevailing westerly winds. We students of the early seventies knew that the student protest movement of the 60s was finished, and we were sorry at our late-bornness. We looked enthusiastically for an excuse to yet express some outrage. This test would do, as we passionately believed we were all quite authentically against the U.S. involvement in Vietnam.

On the test day, classes were canceled at both the Universities of Winnipeg and Manitoba. We watched anti-American films, most notably a less than accurate and completely unflattering piece about Richard M. Nixon called Millhouse. At noon we marched down to the American Consulate at #6 Donald Street and started to state our opinion against the test, against the evil American Imperialist, and only slightly secretly, we stated our yen for a demonstration that would place us in infamy forever in the ranks of the Chicago Seven, Abbie Hoffman, and the rest of our anti-establishment heroes. We found ourselves among hundreds, maybe even thousands, of singing, fist-raising, snowball-throwing "radicals" marching in a huge circle all around the Consulate. Strangely and warmly, it felt more like a party than an angry happening. Then the police came.

In the early seventies, the Winnipeg police wore buffalo coats in the winter, and I remember that few of them seemed to stand less than seven feet tall. Their snap arrival, quick deployment, and ordered queuing on the Consulate steps with arms folded in front and riot sticks at their sides changed the atmosphere in an instant. A collective shudder ran through the crowd, and for the first time all day we felt fear, and we felt anger. We also began to know how the psychology of a crowd could be turned from fun into fire. For a moment that seemed longer, the circle of chanting students stopped, frozen. A self-styled Marxist-Leninist from the University took to the lower step of the Consulate within reach of the nearest policeman, and raised a megaphone to his mouth. A reformer and an activist, he could see a moment in history and he seized it. "Should we storm the doors?" he shouted, hoping for a profoundly revolutionary answer and suggesting, of course, that we should be overrunning the police now in place precisely to stop such an act. We, the crowd, made no answer. The activist repeated his call:

"Should we storm the door?"

"Yes!" came the roar of the crowd.

The policemen put their hands on their sticks.

"Why should we storm the doors?" bellowed the inciter.

The cold Winnipeg air was silent again, for the second time. The question rolled through the winter air a second time: "Why should we storm the doors?"

And then, from somewhere way in the back of the crowd, cutting through the winter crisp air, came a lone high-pitched voice, "Because it's cold out here!"

That ended the thing. The police stepped down. We laughed, threw a few lackluster and puffy snowballs, and headed back for the University with its hot chocolate and beer.

The passing of youth is a frightening thing. It takes the fight out of life. When shouting looks like

62

it might become punching, it's just better to go home. We got our demonstration though. Some day it will tell well to our kids. And even better to theirs.

What do we want? What do we want people to remember about us? I know that we students wanted a piece of history that day, we wanted a demonstration. But I don't think we wanted any violence. But our not wanting any violence wasn't because we were so ideologically against it; we were against it because we were more timid than assertive, more fainthearted than brave. From what does the courage to be come? And what are we courageous about? Some of our missionary friends will not leave one of the most dangerous corners of the world despite guns to their heads and having to lock up their daughters against the crazy roving bands of wild young men carrying guns and looking for sport. Some of us won't utter a word about God to anyone, but we'll take on someone 40 pounds our superior if we're wearing skates and carrying a hockey stick. I wonder what God thinks as he looks down on us selectively loving, selectively seeking justice, selectively carrying our crosses. Is he amused, sometimes? Disgusted? Amazed? We must so often seem so close, but yet so far away from catching on to the bare minimum we need to know in order to live as we should.

The nuclear fallout, the butt flicked out of the car window, the tons of paper wrappings around our food, and the gas burned to just look at stuff we don't need anyway, all show that we are vandals of this earth more than we are good stewards. That God would entrust us with this globe and all its resources should humble us to amazement at his faith. We are outraged when a street kid runs a key down the side of our new Lexus; I wonder if God registers the same incredulity as we continually scratch the world.

On odd occasions some of us cautiously lend out some of our most prized possessions, but if we see that they are being misused, we snatch them back posthaste. God made a paradise; dropped humankind smack in the best center of it, and we started screwing it up immediately. God sent his Son to set us straight; we killed him. All these years later, God in his abundant patience still waits for us to smarten up. We can talk about God's graciousness quite glibly; there is nothing glib about the grace of God. He hangs on when none of us would put up with such behavior from our own creations for a moment. People are dying in the way, poison is spreading across the land, and we make a party of it, singing and dancing as if nothing is amiss. I don't think we're all that cute; I don't think God gives us what we deserve. He lets us off, waiting, waiting for a new day of awareness when we'll see it all and finally say, "My God and my redeemer." I'm not sure we've got much time. But the time, I suspect, is short because we just might make this place uninhabitable before morning. In the meantime, it seems that God's patience is interminable and his grace unending. His voice in calling out in the cold that we can come into his warmth.

Vicki

I'd heard about Vicki long before I met her. Her distraught friends wept openly and talked about their friend with leukemia in my class-room. The next year she showed up in my class, and we became friends. She talked about dying; I talked about life.

One day Vicki suggested to our counselors that the school should host a student seminar on death and dying. The seminar drew a hundred nervous but wide-eyed teenagers. When the seminar leader, the local hospital chaplain, asked who in the room was not afraid to die, only Vicki, the only one knowing she had terminal cancer, stood up.

Through the next few weeks she wasn't at school. We heard reports of horrifying chemo treatments and graft versus host disease before, finally, a good remission brought Vicki bouncing back to school, with a wig and a new zest for life.

We resumed our talks over lunch hours and snatched breaks in crowded hallways. We talked on and on. We laughed and cried. She wrote her papers. I marked them. Life seemed to normalize. Then one day, Vicki grabbed my arm as we met in the hallway teeming with high schoolers. "It's back!" she said.

"What's back?" I asked.

"My leukemia. It's back!"

I stood still in the hallway. I started to weep. Vicki took my hand, and said softly, "It's OK. It's OK," feeling sorry for me. The milling masses of students around us wondered at what was going on. No one said anything.

Vicki's hair grew back and she fought on.

"I know why I was born now, sir," she said, one

day after class, "I was born to get cancer and to help as many people as possible cope with it before it takes me. We're so afraid of cancer that it kills us the minute we hear we have it. The fear of cancer is far worse than the disease. We're all going to die some day. Some of us sooner; some of us later. I'm just one of them that's going to be sooner. It's really not such a big deal!" she added.

"If I don't make it, will you speak at my funeral?"

I guess I answered with my eyes. I couldn't speak.

We didn't see Vicki much after that. They took her to Vancouver, and again we heard of her amazing ability to comfort others in the children's cancer ward. Soon, however, the reports changed. Excruciating canker sores. Endless vomiting. Numbing fatigue.

There was a light knock on my classroom door. I opened the door still talking, still lecturing about some significant historical event somewhere in the world. "You'd better give them something to do, Dan," said the counselor. "I need to talk to you in my office."

I dreaded the news, knowing what it was from the counselor's eyes. Up in the office, she told me that Vicki had just died.

"Vicki's mom called. She wanted me to tell you and some of her school friends. She wonders if you will be available to talk to her on the phone this afternoon?"

The call came. We wept together across 500 miles of telephone connection as Vicki's mom felt the mixing of a terrible loss with relief that a child's suffering was over. "And oh," she said suddenly, "would you consider saying something at Vicki's memorial service?"

"Yes. And I know already what I will say. Vicki and I already talked about this."

At the service we mourned the loss of a young

life, of a good friend, of a daughter. The hospital chaplain, the same one of the death and dying seminar, said that we were here to mourn, we were here to cry. Perhaps it would be good if we just took a few minutes to cry. And we cried. We cried out-loud. We sobbed and we wailed. Our shoulders shook and we held each other. We wept and we wondered. And when we were finished, we were empty and just a little OK.

An hour later some of us stood in Vicki's home with her mom, looking through the doorway into her bedroom. Her room looked like she could come home any moment and resume her existence.

We smiled about her. We laughed about some of her jokes, some of her foibles, her wonderful stubbornness. I think and speak of her often.

It's a mystery how some people are so adept at living, while others seem to fail so miserably. I see that adeptness at life, that ability to be an artist at life, more often around death than I do around the other big passages in life. I almost never see it around weddings or graduations, but I see it when death is at the door, or has already invaded the home. But I do see it sometimes in the work-a-day world of some of the authentically rich people I have known. And when one adds up the ingredients of the artist at life it soon shows that life is not all about intelligence, nor luck, nor good breeding, nor divine favor. It's about a sense of unity with the universe, its rhythms, its direction. It is about love, acceptance, and forgiveness.

Healing the Hapless

The Driver

On Sundays I hitch-hike–if I miss the bus. And on Sundays the buses come once every half hour. It was minus 28 and windy the last time I missed the bus. I stuck my thumb out in the wind and waited. What must have been the last '68 Oldsmobile left in the whole city came heading south in the median lane, its front fenders seemingly flapping like wings, the rust having nearly separated them from the car body itself. The driver saw me shivering in the wind with my hand out before I could react to the wreck barreling south on Pembina and pretend I wasn't begging for a ride that day. He yanked the wheel towards the curb, when he was nearly opposite me, and by the time he had the huge 'boat' corralled and wrestled to the curb, the Oldsmobile was 75 feet down the road beyond me. Hitchhikers usually run to get in cars that stop to pick them up. I sort of sauntered towards the mighty machine that seemed to hang over its wheels, shaking and wheezing, obviously near its final run. I opened the huge door and bent over to engage the driver. Smoke rolled out past his 'roll yer own' cigarette, curled over his yellow-brown, tobacco-stained bottom lip and out his nose. The driver gestured towards me over a great bundle of newspapers and a cardboard box piled high with empty liter oil cans from the heaving monster's last oil change on the front seat beside him. I should get in, his gestures invited. Or was it, demanded?

"Just a minute!" the driver shouted, as he began throwing flapping newspapers with bright glossy inserts and dripping oil cans into the cavernous back-half of the car, adding to an increasing world of back seat helter-skelter. The front seat now cleared, the driver hit it with his fist, indicating where I could sit. His friendliness permeated the smoke in the car and seemed to warm the frigid air. I slid onto the front seat of that throbbing monster, wondering about my good coat, about how much oil had soaked into the car seat and now waited for me to blot up. I was buttoned to the throat, no tie proceeded above the collar. I carried no Bible.

"You goin' to church?" shouted the driver, assuming, I guess, that I was nearly deaf, and somehow mysteriously knowing I was on my way to church.

"Yeah," I said.

"Don't you just hate it when you're late for church? Gee, that used to brown me off when I was late for church. Nothin' wrecks a good service like bein' late. It used to make me so mad, so, so, uh...!" And his voice trailed off muttering and fuming wildly ironic and ungodly expletives about how angry he got when he was late for Sunday morning services.

"Where's your church?" he interrupted himself.

"Just a ways up, right on Pembina."

"Don't you worry, young fella, I'll get you there on time. Nothin' I hate worse than bein' late for church. I could just ...."

"Turn in here!" I pointed. "You coming in? You'd be on time!"

"Nope, can't make it today. Would sure like to though. God bless you, young man; not many your age goin' to church anymore, it seems. Too bad! Blessings, boy!"

I slammed the door, and the Oldsmobile and its just-as-large-as-life driver roared and hurled itself out towards the highway. It swung onto Pembina without a stop, without the driver even checking the traffic, I think, to see whether anyone else was coming. South it streaked in its magnificent broken glory, the pedal to the floor. The driver seemed in a hurry. I guess he was late for church somewhere else.

What do we do with a guy who swears like a sailor, even takes God's name in vain, but says he loves the Church? Do we silently and maybe politely guffaw at the contradiction and stick to our church-learned definitions? Or do we become curious about him and try to find out how his life, to him, is lived in a straight line?

Why would the driver lie to me about liking church? I'm nothing to him. Why would he say such things?

I think he was being honest. He does like church, or at least he likes what he remembers of church. He just doesn't get to be there as often as he thinks he would like to. I think the driver was more honest, in fact, than many of us who never miss church, who wouldn't dream of missing church, but really live our lives in meanness, slander and gossip. Some of the most spiritual people I know are in the church; some of the most hateful are there also. Some of the deepest people I know go for quiet walks on Sunday mornings and will only be caught dead in a church; some of the shallowest are in leadership positions in the church. Some of the most spiritual people never come to sing hymns and worship songs, or hear a good sermon; some of the least spiritual don't ever take a Sunday off for a holiday, and they are careful to shout, "Amen!" at all the right moments.

I'm glad that God in his wisdom knows the truth and isn't fooled by anyone. He has perfect, total insight into our beings. I also know, though, that God seeks with the same intensity the driver screaming around a frozen city thinking it's time to get back to Church, as he does the regular who snores through the sermon and blesses God in his private prayers that he is not like others.

The little BIG Man

They were a trinity of dwarfs, three short, real short people: a man and two women. The man and the younger lady nearly as wide as high, and the older woman bent over. Way over. Her spine resembled a stick bent too much that broke one day and then just stayed "lookin' over" forever.

We saw the trio on the street a few times before they appeared in our church one Sunday. They shuffled down the street, pulling a wagon filled with bottles and papers and groceries, and they could always be seen to be talking, talking, always talking. Even from a passing car, one could tell that something was odd and unusual about this group. The little chap always walked along in front of the two women, more like he was riding shotgun and protecting his own possessions than he was protecting the women. Not, I found out later, that they ever needed his protection, though some protection they could have used. Somehow, in spite of his smallness, he exuded a warning of his control, of his power. And then one day they came to church.

Now without being snobby, we were a middle-class church, not pretentious or anything, but we were people successful enough, and a lot of students. Poor students who somehow already lived the life of what their professional careers would one day earn them, and not many of them poor, really. So the trio didn't fit in. Not only were all three of them smaller than every adult in the place, but their look, their aura, their everything reflected an otherworldliness. A world not like ours; a world none of us really wanted to know. And yet we couldn't put our finger on what made them different, but everybody, I think, all five hundred of us that day, knew that they were there. Something about them made us feel guilty.

I saw the short man heading for me even before my benedictory "Amen!" had stopped echoing around the nave and back from the balcony window at the end of the service. I think I instinctively knew the little man would feed his self-importance on making my acquaintance. Something about being pastor can foolishly feed the ego often enough, but sometimes some of it and someone makes us clergymen wish we could fall through a trap door after the benediction and simply not talk to anyone. The "thank you" is good, the "I enjoyed that sermon," is confusing, but the need to chat up the Reverend for all to see is clearly asinine. I hated it then and I still do. And I hated it no more than on this day when this little man shuffled up to me, a devilish grin on his face, his hand pulling himself toward me at a near run, reminiscent of TV sitcom Taxi's Louie after his latest feminine fantasy.

I found out his name and learned that he lived in the complex down the road from the church with his wife and his daughter. He introduced his daughter; he forgot about his wife. She stood, hunched over, not expecting to be introduced, not wanting to anyway, probably, I guessed.

The two social workers in our congregation, the one retired, phoned me the afternoon of that first visit. They had both handled a file on this family in times past; they were both agitated. I became curious.

After that initial Sunday, this little new family came to the morning service every week. They sat near the front of the sanctuary. The husband, the dad, joined in the service with more than just a little enthusiasm. No one sang like this little scalawag; no one prayed like this little leprechaun. The zeal, the passion, and the pious phrases pouring forth from our newest adherent should have warmed any pastor wanting to grow a church. Involuntarily, I shuddered. I hoped no one noticed. Forgive me, Lord!

The grinning gnome became my friend. It was my job to be everyone's friend. Pastors are supposed to befriend everyone who comes in the place. It seemed that everyone else skirted widely this peculiar trinity in the foyer. The little guy went around greeting like a deacon. The daughter with bright red lipstick painted on wider than her lips stood with her dad, and waited for him to signal when it was time to go home. The little mother just looked at the carpet.

Sundays passed from week to week and the tiny threesome became regulars. At any opportunity given for a story to be shared, or a testimony to be spilled, the little gentleman shouted it out with tears and confessions and a thesaurus worth of churchy clichés. The "sharing" discomforted the congregation more than it ministered. The congregation looked down in embarrassment at its own embarrassment. The listeners felt like the crowd telling Zacchaeus to shut up and come down from the tree. When I called for prayers of commitment, the little man toddled to the front, alone, knelt on the carpeted stairway and swayed out his muttered renewals like a Lubavitcher Jew at the Wailing Wall. I tried to get some of the senior members to take him for coffee, talk to him. They shied away. I wondered what Jesus would do with this man.

It was one early weeknight winter evening, but dark already, that the story changed. It was cold out. Minus 20 or so. Suddenly, the daughter was at the locked door of the church hammering with both fists. She was disheveled and coatless. Some of her bright lipstick was smeared up the side of her face, its redness mingled with the thick layer of orangy pancake foundation she always wore on special occasions. I pushed open the door, grasped her wrist and sped her through the foyer and into my office. I closed the door. "It's too awful. He... He... He...!" she cried.

She was interrupted by the sound of someone shouting and kicking the door before she could even begin to tell her story. Leaving her, I stepped into the foyer in front of my office and by instinct I called out in the foyer the name of one of the biggest college guys who I knew was in one of the other offices. As we moved toward the door we could see the little man through the glass door pulled up to his full height, looking more than just a little threatening. I opened the door a few inches.

"Is my daughter in there?" he shouted.

"Yes!"

"I want her to come home immediately!"

"No!" I started to say as he crouched and dove to get past us. I caught the flying fury with my hip and pushed him up against the door post. My volunteer help pushed the two of us, enraged father and pacifist but pugilistic pastor out through the doorway and onto the snowy steps. Then my hired muscle and I pushed the writhing and cursing little man down onto the frozen landing with considerable struggle until he finally stopped kicking. Realizing his powerlessness, the enraged attacker instantly changed his approach and asked if we couldn't have a civilized conversation. "We would have to have that conversation in your office, though," he added. I declined his offer. With no way to get into the church to find his daughter, and with no way to get past us two "giants," he dismissed us with a curse and scurried back through the snow to his apartment building.

The horror story that spilled from the daughter appalled us. We couldn't stop her story tirade of abuse visited upon abuse at the hands of her father. I found her a safe house for the night. She stayed two days. Then she called her dad to come take her home.

Every time I get the not so uncommon news that abused daughters keep going back to their tormentors, I confess that there are times I curse, and then I weep. Sometimes I hate this world; sometimes I can't even pray. Sometimes I'm glad I don't have God's power. Because if I did, I'd hurt someone. I am powerless all over the place in these abuse stories, and I ask the questions: Could I have loved these people to health? Could I have taught this congregation to touch and try to heal these people? Sometimes I feel I don't know anything, and in between it feels like I do nothing.

I think I understand how a loving God withholds his hand when nations rage against one another with smart bombs, guided missiles and indestructible tanks, but I wonder at his patience when he doesn't stop the publicly pious father who secretly and forever desecrates a daughter: her sexuality, her spirit and her soul.

Does the comforting Spirit whisper to her in the midst of all that injustice that justice will come another day, enough to help a little girl feel not so abandoned? Does the comforting Spirit reassure her that she will be okay someday in the arms of someone who really loves her, really wants what is best for her?

Our great God withheld his hand one day when all the power of earth pushed his son around, when liars blamed him for everything though he had done nothing to warrant any blame, and when the crowds concocted a story, a religious story, of course, about how he, the son, had blasphemed the Father. How would they know? Since when does God need human judges, human soldiers, human lawyers, or human journalists to decide whether somebody is blasphemous or not? The very act of deciding that someone is blaspheming is probably in itself already blasphemous. But God, the Father, stood back and interfered not when they spit on him, nor when they drove the nails through human flesh with human sensibilities. I think there must be times when God's spirit eyes are clouded with tears. But he holds back his hand. Why? Because he loves. To snatch his son from the hands of the cruel spitters and slappers, taunters and tyrants, would have left all of humankind without a way home, without a way to eternal life. Every time the Father must have wanted to reach down and vaporize a pious killer or zap a Roman soldier, I think he must have seen us someday trying to swim towards a shore that was too far away and humanly impossible to reach, so he stayed his hand and let them have their way with Jesus. God sees justice, sees life on the big screen, in the long term. Short term solutions to even horrific events must be like not finishing the antibiotics; the disease comes back stronger than ever. So God holds on. I don't know how he holds on, for his ways are largely incomprehensible to me, but he does hold on. He holds on, graciously. I can learn to trust him more than myself. He, God, Creator, Changer—maker of good things to come out of bad, Forgiver, Understander, is bigger than I am little.

Gabriel

Something like a shadow–cutting off the light coming in my open door from the bright foyer– caught my attention. I looked up from my writing to see a tall dark man framed in the doorway.

"Hi," he said, "I'm Gabriel."

"Well, hello," I answered. "I've been waiting for you. But I expected more, more—light." I gestured towards him, drawing an aura in the air around him.

"I'm really hammered," he volunteered.

"Do you need some coffee or breakfast?" I asked.

"Yeah, I could sure use some. I'm out of cash. I hit the old lady and I'm out on the street. She won't let me back in. Well, actually, I'm a little scared to go back there. Maybe after a cup of coffee."

I grabbed my jacket and said, "Let's go!"

We crossed Pembina Highway. Behaving like a guardian angel, I had to grab Gabriel's arm to stop him from lurching out in front of the cars heading downtown. We found a table for two, and Gabriel got busy scouting the room for a smoke. I couldn't tell whether he was more charming than drunk, or more drunk than charming. With perfect timing, he bummed a cigarette from a woman after he lit one up for her, using her lighter. By the time he had his own lit, she had decided to give him the rest of her pack, and he pocketed her lighter.

Gabriel headed back to our table. "Coffee or breakfast?" I asked.

"I think I should have some breakfast."

"What do you want?"

"Anything you order. You're smart," he said.

I ordered breakfast and started in on Gabriel. I

felt unusually familiar with this stranger.

"What's the deal, Gabriel? Why are you so drunk at nine in the morning? You talked about the 'old lady'. Did you do something stupid?"

"Yeah, she caught me with another woman in the alley, and she screamed at me. I hate that when she yells at me. So I drifted her one. She fell down and I think I kicked her a couple of times. I don't know what happened after that. Are you a minister?"

"Yes, I'm a minister. But your wife, your girlfriend? Where is she now?"

"She's back in the apartment. I walked all the way from downtown. I asked some cops to give me a ride, but you know them cops don't help Indians. Nah, you wouldn't know that. I'm scared to go home now. The old lady will throw me out. You know I love Jesus. I shouldn't do this stuff. Booze and fight. But I can't help it. I get so teed-off!"

"Guys who love Jesus shouldn't go hitting their women, Gabriel. Where do you live?"

"By your fruits you shall know them, eh?" he laughed, a northern Ontario native accent rolling off his tongue. I couldn't really see whether his eyes sparkled or whether they were dead like so many others I had met on the street. His seemed to shift and change. Sometimes they were dark; sometimes they were bright.

"I'm Pentecostal, Reverend," he drawled, spitting out the Reverend like a challenge–I didn't know whether he was respecting me or mocking me–"and I bet I know more Bible verses than you do, but, gee, why do I hit the old lady and get like this? Aw, I don't care! Who cares anyway? What difference does any of it make? You don't smoke, do you? Never met a good preacher that does, though I've shared a good drink with some, I have, I have."

"Eat your breakfast; it's getting cold, Gabriel."

"Don't white man me with your directions, you.

Why did I hit her? It's harder for a drunk to get to heaven than a camel to get through a needle eye. Pretty good, eh? Do you think they've got more coffee? That woman gave me nearly a whole pack of smokes, you know. There's still some good folks. You're a good folk, you know!" He laughed. At himself, I think.

"What does your wife, or girl friend do, that you're living down here on Pembina?" I asked.

"She goes to university. She's studying to be a lawyer. Can you believe that? An Indian woman, a lawyer?"

"You hit a woman? And a woman who is studying to be a lawyer? Gabriel, are you nuts?"

"Nah. Stupid. Just drunk stupid. Do you think she'll let me back? She should give me another chance, shouldn't she? I'll quit drinking. I don't like it anyway. Ah, she's such a bag anyway. I've hit lots of women. Doesn't matter, does it? Turn the other cheek, that's what Jesus taught 'em. I wonder if she'll walk another mile with me? Or give me her second coat? The cops wouldn't give me a ride. This is good breakfast. Oh look. The woman who gave me the cigarettes is leaving– 'Jesus loves you, ma'am! Thanks again!'"

"What are you going to do, Gabriel?" I interjected.

"I don't know. I think it's probably over with this old lady after this. Guess I'll head back to Ontario. Get straightened out. Quit drinking. I'm still drunk, you know. Jesus drank. Not this much, though. I don't think he hit anyone, either. You're a good man. I know everything you preach. I could even teach you some things. I'm a Christian. Memorized all of I Corinthians once. Want to hear it? 'Paul, called to be an apostle of Christ Jesus by the will of God and our brother Sosthenes, To the church of God in Corinth'–I like Romans better. It's harder to understand. I gotta go!"

"Gabriel. If you want to talk, you know where I am. In my office waiting for angels..."

"Nah, talk, talk. I'm sick of talkin".

As we headed for the door, he reached up to the plastic flowers braided into a kind of K-Mart display on top the buffet server. He twisted off a dusty rose, handed it to me, "This is for you, God bless, preacher!"

And he was gone. I really don't know where he went. When I looked up from the stolen flower he had pressed into my hand, I couldn't see him. I paid for the breakfast and hurried out into the street. Pembina is a wide and open street, but he wasn't anywhere. Neither north nor south.

This Gabriel. What was he? An angel? A drunk? A fallen angel? A lost soul? A good man? An abuser? Somebody's dad? A lover? A charmer? A nuisance? All of these, Lord? And more? And what has this got to do with me? Something, Lord, I know that. But you'll have to tell me what! And Lord, hold Gabriel. For someone, for me, because I can't. I can't find him.

It's confusing, sometimes, how contradictory some things, some people, are. Life would be a lot simpler if everything, no matter how good or bad, was more consistent, more predictable. How do we understand a man who knows the Bible, and certainly the essence of its truth, and then completely misuses it? At first flash, Gabriel is an exceptional character, but then really he's no different than most of us. If we're not contradictory, somewhat conflicting in our behavior we're not very human.

I don't know if we live our lives attempting to stop being contradictory, or if it's all a huge attempt to come to some understanding and acceptance that the contradictions are simply the dialectic of human existence.

God is gracious; he is also judge. We must be very

careful to not see humans, nor their Creator, as uni-dimensional. We are not a flat piece of paper born clean or white that gets its experiences scribbled on it in varying shades. We are more like a soccer ball with a multitude of panels that are like but unlike one another, all living at their own angle to the whole. No panel is any less authentic than the others, each panel must live in integrity in order to be true to the Creator.

Gabriel is a lost soul and, at times, an abuser, a human vandal; he is also an attractive person with enough charm to win him friends anywhere. To be powerful is to walk in the image of God, but the destruction comes from elsewhere. To be warm and inviting is to walk in the image of God, as well, but to be manipulative and inauthentic comes from else-where, too. Some of us may not live as destructively as Gabriel does, but there are moments when he reflects the delightfulness of his Creator more than the most righteous person we may have ever met. Behind the self-hate and the bloodied eyes, the violence and the booze, the Bible verses and the charm, lives Gabriel, whom God loves as much as he loves Billy Graham.

In the same way that Gabriel cannot be put into a descriptive box, even less-so can God be nailed down. He can be described, and then there is more. He can be understood, but only partially. His behavior can be predicted, and then what he does next is utterly sur-prising. I stand in awe at how mysterious are the crea-tures who crawl this earth with me; I am simply amazed at the creativity of the Creator who made us. His imagination is his drawing board; the light over his table is his love and his delight is his people working their way towards being more and more like him. I am not distressed by Gabriel and all his contradictions, though I am saddened. Gabriel has the world at his fingertips; he has been given by the Creator all he needs to live a life that touches wholeness in others and himself. Will he waste it or utilize it? Will we?

The Pactmaker

A friend of a friend called from Vancouver.
"I don't know anyone in Winnipeg and my uncle and aunt in the North End are in real trouble. She's dying of cancer, and he's drinking heavily. I think they've made a pact that when she dies, he'll kill himself. At least that's what he says. Will you call my Uncle Joe? I'll give you his number."

Now I don't usually, in fact, I don't ever call people to counsel them. Not much point. But my caller begged me to call his uncle. I waited a day and then called. The house was full of relatives, one of the cousins answered, and, yes, Auntie was dying, and Joe, well, he was drunk, and raving. I said I was a clergyman and that I had been called by relatives in Vancouver to see if I could do something.

"Do they need someone to come and sit with them through this? Could I speak to Joe?" Joe came to the phone. Composed, rational, charming, actually, he didn't sound drunk at all. He apologized for the bother he was to me, a total stranger, and, no, they didn't need me to come over. The relatives in Vancouver were just a little panicky, he thought. I volunteered to come and sit with them if they wanted, but that I would not if they didn't ask. We said good-bye.

It was one in the morning when the phone jangled me out of a deep sleep. One of the cousins begged me to come. Auntie was indeed dying and Joe was really crazy. He was letting no one into the room with her, and the sisters were sneaking in to be with her when every-so-often he dipped into the basement to take long pulls at yet another Jack Daniels. They said there were dozens of empties down there, littering the whole basement. I promised that I would come, remembering that it was Saturday night and tomorrow would be a big day for me at the church. Sundays always are. Bigger for sure than God had ever intended, I often thought.

I drove through the core of the city away from my safe suburban neighborhood bright with middle class Christmas light order, and warmth. Drunks, reeling on the curbs with bare hands and hatless heads in the subzero weather playing roulette with death by alcohol numbing unawareness, suggested a foreshadowing of what was ahead of me, somewhere in a strange house on a snowplowed street. I found the house and parked, telling myself I had better not forget to come out from time to time to restart the car in this hellish cold. I knocked on the door and shuddered. I don't think it was only the cold that caused the shudder.

The cousin opened the door, shook my hand and greeted me warmly. I think he was glad he didn't know me, or I him. It was less shameful this way. I was introduced to Joe, who was reeling by on his way to his basement drink. He very politely shook my hand, apologized to my high calling for all the inconvenience, and excused himself to the basement. A couple of women, almost tripping over each other, hurried me into a back bedroom to talk to their dying Auntie while Joe was in the basement. "Could I do something? Give last rites or something? Quick, before Joe comes back. He's not letting any of us talk to her anymore. Do something! Quick!"

Auntie was dying. That was sure. A barely skin-covered skeleton stared up at the ceiling. Her hair was wispy and thin, very thin, her high forehead was wrinkled and endless. Her skin was dark as if unnaturally tanned or maybe malnourished. Her dark eyes, huge and desperate and feverish like the eyes of an injured deer on the roadside, were beautiful. They shone their light of life into the awfulness of the scene, and I think she could see me. For a moment I forgot the ugliness of this demonic house and its silent death threat screaming about the rooms. I could only see the beauty of this woman staring upwards. I think reaching out to me. Or was she reaching out for God? Some people actually think that's who a clergyman is. God! I felt affection for her. And warmth. I put my cheek against hers and I talked in her ear.

"If you can hear me, Alice, please know you are loved. And your God, Jesus, he loves you amazingly. If you wish to be with him, just say 'Yes!' to him. If you can't say, 'Yes!' just think it and squeeze my hand. It will be all good with Jesus, and it won't hurt anymore. Just go with him. He's calling you. And Joe? Don't worry about him. We'll look after him well. Sleep, Aunt Alice, sleep, go with Jesus. I'll pray. 'Oh, Lord, hear this beautiful woman saying 'Yes!' to your calling and take her to yourself where everything is wonderful. Where there is no cancer. Where there is no pain. Where there is no trouble. Let her come home to you, Jesus; set her free. In Christ's name, Amen!'"

"He's coming! Get out of there!" shouted the sister at the door, a desperate and urgent panic invading the serenity of the room. I stepped out to meet Joe.

"What you doin', Reverend? What you doin' with my sweetheart?" He pounced on the bed and took up Alice like a life-size rag doll, her head falling back. "Don't leave me! Don't leave me, darlin'!" Joe screamed. "You can't leave me. I'm comin' with you." He laid her back, suddenly gentle, and sobbing, he lay down beside her. He passed out.

I sat in the living room with the sisters, the cousins and the in-laws. One small lamp burned in the corner. In the semi-darkness I learned of Joe and

Alice. These people, these storytellers, they loved her; they hated him. They were disgusted at his behavior; they feared his power. I heard of Joe and Alice's marriage. Of their devotion. Of his dependency. Of his domineering. Of his lunacy. Of his drinking. Of her loveliness. Of her warmth and long-suffering. We talked for hours.

Her sisters looked into the room from time to time, but they could not go close. Joe lay still, his back to the elongated but beloved hump under the blanket beside him. Just a long hump with eyes staring up at the ceiling from the midst of a pillow. I tiptoed to her side. I took her hand. It was too stiff. Too coolish. I felt for a pulse in her wrist. Nothing. I felt for a life-telling throb in her neck. Nothing. I put my ear to her lips, hoping for a whistle, or even a rattle. Nothing.

I stepped out to the doorway and peered into the half light. All the eyes pleaded with me more than looked at me.

"She's gone!" I said, "Alice is gone."

A scream rose in the house. "She's dead? Turn on the lights! Turn on the lights! Joe, Joe, she's gone. Alice is gone."

It seemed that the whole house convulsed. Joe rose on the bed with a roar. He screamed at the body finally released, "No! No!" He clutched her toward himself. He shook her. "Don't go. Don't go! Sweetheart. Sweetheart!"

"Joe! Joe!" I said, "she's gone. It's over. The thing's done. She's not suffering anymore."

"I'm comin' too, darlin', I'm comin' too!" Joe lunged off the bed, nearly fell, and headed for the bathroom, ripping at his pocket. I saw a bottle of pills in his hand just as he rounded the corner for the door.

"Get in after him," I yelled. "Don't let him get in the bathroom alone. He's going to take the pills. Harry, quick, get in there with him. Someone call

911. Harry, get into the bathroom with Joe."

"I can't go into the bathroom with Uncle Joe!" whined a terrified Harry.

"Just get in there and make sure he doesn't take those pills. Do whatever you have to do, Harry, but make sure he doesn't take those pills," I yelled. As I got my foot in the closing door, I pushed a frightened Harry through the doorway into Joe's bathroom, knocking the older man against the wall. Joe cursed. It looked like Harry would stay. Suddenly, a wild-eyed shouting clergyman was more to be obeyed than a drunken and cursing uncle was to be feared. I ran to the phone.

For once they must have been just around the corner. First, the First Response team. Then the blue coats and ambulance attendants. Two policemen nearly broke Joe's wrist twisting the bottle of pills out of his hand, while the medics wildly tried to revive Auntie Alice.

Joe was madder at Harry than he was at the police. The people from the Coroner's office who take away the bodies arrived. Joe swore around the house, cursing everybody, declaring his resolve to join Alice as he had promised, and soon.

The relatives were disgusted. Frightened of cancer; angry at death. They could have killed Joe, however. That would have been easy. Is death always easier than indignity?

I got home around six a.m. Slept a little. Got up to get ready for church. The theme of the sermon was death. I wondered what it was I had written through the week before this last night. Would any of it ring true now?

Joe phoned me today. He says the relatives are angry about his behavior at the funeral. He wonders what their problem is. He wants to know whether I think he did okay.

Somebody once said, "The human condition dictates that we die the way we live!" I don't begin to know all the wisdom that statement might hold or point to, but in the strange mixture of life and death that night in that home, I'm not sure I could tell the one from the other. Alice wanting to live, I think, but having to die; and Joe, wanting to die, having to live. The family, in that moment of death, by their love wished they could bring Alice back to life, and by their disgust wished they could send Joe to his death.

Jesus, living in that sometimes bizarre land-bridge of the world, caught between Europe, Asia and Africa, watched as the whole world ran through his community. He could see greed and degradation, he could see caring and tenderness, but mostly he saw lostness. He wept over a city doomed, and he reached out to the sick and the dying, the weak and the repulsive. He screamed at money traders, criticized the exploiters of the simply religious, and scathingly confronted the self-righteously religious, but spoke gently to hookers. He often said that the first shall be last, and the last shall be first. In other words, he said that winners will be losers and that losers will be winners. This should all be a little frightening for those of us who are winners here. Makes one wonder what side of the scoreboard we'll be on when God draws up and marks the final paper.

Alice was a winner in the eyes of her family, but she died; Joe was a loser in those same eyes, but he lived. I'd be interested in watching Jesus' eyes looking at the two of them. When he reached out to both of them, and he would reach out to both of them–what would he say–what would he zero in on as their need?

Alice was beautiful, even in death, I could see that, and Joe, well, he's a likable old guy. I feel sorry for him. He's really not that huggable of a type, unshaven, bloodshot-eyed and smelly and all, but he is lovable. He is lovable. That's how God sees him. And us, too, no matter what. He made that pact. He covenants to be our God as he called and he calls us to be his people regardless of who we are or even what we've done.

Fostered by Family

Jake

We lived out in the country, miles from town in a locale where the traffic passing by our place would leave a sleeping dog lie most of its days. When, however, that one car a week did pass by, we all stopped our hoeing, hammering, washing, peeling, fixing, playing, or sleeping just to see whose car was passing by. We needed to know who had been so lucky to have gone to town this week. Our house was sheltered by a thick row of Manitoba maples on the west, making any vehicle coming from that way noticeable at first only by the roar of its mufflers, and the din and clamor of gravel on the inside of its fenders. When cars did come from the west we waited, hushed, until their metal beauty emerged from behind the big bush northwest of our house and passed into magnificent view directly in front of our house, just 200 meters away across the big slough. I seldom saw those rare and infrequent cars, however. For just as they were about to come into view, my big brother would catch me in a headlock, drive my cherub face into the unseeing grass, and marvel:

"The Dueck boys have put Imperial lights on their new '58 Monarch! And fender-skirts!"

"Look at the fins on that '59 Plymouth!"

My face at the end of my writhing and threatening puny body stayed in the dirt until the lights, the fins, and the fender-skirts were just a cloud of dust chasing all that wonder and the highlight of the week down the road into the fading east.

I vowed that one day I would be bigger than he, and then he would writhe with his face in the grass. But I never did get big enough. Boy, I loved that big brother. I still do.

God is strong and cannot be controlled by us. All of us exercise our fallenness , more or less, by trying to control others. And we use everything we've got: our size, our sex, our voice, our status, our position, our knowledge, our expertise, our charm, our anger, our silence, our money, our poverty, our diseases, our habits, our handicaps. We make our weaknesses our strengths, if they can get us what we want. We use whatever we can, often more unconsciously than consciously. And God watches. What must he think? I wonder how differently we would behave if we knew that others knew, and we knew what our real motives were?

Imagine being strong, so strong that you feel no compunction to use that power, because you have no needs. God is needless. He doesn't need our praise and worship; he has no ego-need that we lie on our faces before him. Then why does he call for it? Because we need it. For if we don't fall on our faces before him, we fall on our faces before ourselves. And if we fall on our faces before ourselves, we've fallen before something that will trip and topple itself, sooner or later. God has created us somewhat needy, so if we don't find a focus outside ourselves, we'll blow up, so to speak. And if we need a focus beyond ourselves, there is only one being beyond ourselves that is worthy of falling down before, and that is God. A God so powerful, so magnificent, so pure, so hinged, we can't possibly do any better. Beyond that, anything we spend time with, we begin to become a little bit like. Why would we not want to be a little more like God who is egoless, needless?

Tante Nuht

I f it can accurately be said that the colonial British "kept a stiff upper lip!" then it can just as accurately be said that my Germanic fore-bears "kept both lips stiff!" Except for Tante Nuht. Somehow this woman had decided to live her life at breakneck speed, screaming and laughing. She seemed to not even notice that the family tended to the somber. Even the fact that her husband, John, earned his living as coffin maker—and he even had the planning and the foresight to build their own personal caskets that sat out in the shed quietly waiting for 20 years, silently calling—never damp-ened her zest for life.

Tante Nuht and Uncle John came out to visit us on the farm one summer. It was only a few minutes after their arrival in our home before we children knew that we were in for an adventure, an unforget-table relationship with this wild woman in a longish black dress, kerchief, brown stockings rolled to a neat ring just below her knees, and clunky black shoes. Tante Nuht was mousey-looking, with little round granny glasses out in front of squinty eyes that were as unreadable as a poker player's, and white hair pulled tightly back into a severe bun, but there was nothing mousey nor meek about this woman.

On the first day of Tante Nuht's visit she announced her intention to butcher a few chickens from our flock, "For chicken soup as it should be made!" She found a cleaver in the kitchen drawer and herded us kids ahead of her out of the house and toward the barn, looking for her free-ranging barn-yard victims. She didn't have to enlist our help to join her, we had already surmised that this woman was a walking, talking adventure, a pre-Disneyland amusement experience on two legs.

Tante Nuht shrieked at the older kids to catch the visually selected but unwary chickens scratching in the weeds or fluffing around in the little dust pools they create for their own purification, fun, and relaxation. We younger children waited with Tante Nuht by the chopping block, a stump permanently stained dark and red with dried blood across the top and running down the sides. The block was flagged with vestiges of guillotined feathers in and around the slashes and welts of axes that had done their work on hundreds of hens over the past number of years of noodly-good eating at our house.

The chickens scattered out of their routines, flying madly in all directions as the big kids picked on the selected victims and the dog joined in the excitement of the hunt. A plump brown hen, perfect for soup stock, was handed to Tante Nuht. She pulled back its wings around its legs, grasping the feet and the long end wing feathers in one hand, and turned the bird around to examine all its sides. Then pulling the chicken across the top of the block so that its head would be extended out behind its full body, Tante Nuht exposed its neck to the cleaver that she had been sharpening with a stone all the while the chickens had been scouted and caught. With the sudden and piercing scream of a black-belt breaking a board, Tante Nuht raised her killing tool in a high arc over her head and brought the cleaver down and through the neck of the chicken in a clean and vicious swipe. The head shot off the edge of the block as the decapitated body of the chicken convulsed and blood spurted out the pulsating red end where the chicken's head used to be.

Tante Nuht's head came up from the bloody intensity on the block with a delicious grin on her face, and brandishing the bleeding hen in one hand before her, and the upraised bloody cleaver in her other, she chased us screaming from the butcher block and out into the wide barn yard. And we ran. We ran like we had never run before. After all, we had never been chased by a bleeding headless chicken before, nor a woman anything like this. While we suspected that this sparkly-eyed woman felt great affection for us, the grizzly sight and smell of fresh blood and her shouting, threatening wildness sent us scattering in panic.

Later that same evening we were hardly surprised when Tante Nuht chased us around the yard on my brother's bike, swinging a baseball bat over her head, her dress pulled up high enough to not interfere with her peddling.

A few days into Tante Nuht's visit, she and her husband and Mom and Dad stopped their work and got ready to go out. Putting on their "church clothes," neither mother nor father made any fuss about me getting my ears cleaned or my nice clothes on, so I soon realized that I was being left at home with the big kids. I didn't like being left behind so I slammed out through the screen door and locked myself in Dad's green '52 Ford, making sure the keys were in the car with me. I pouted down behind the steering wheel and waited.

It wasn't long before Mom and Dad and Uncle John and Tante Nuht came out of the house. I watched Dad's face as he pulled on the door handle of the car door and I watched his eyes as he realized that the door was locked. About the same time he saw my little face looking up at him through the window glass.

"Open the door, Danny!" he said, not really suspecting my criminal intentions.

I shook my head, "No!"

Puzzled, he ordered again.

"No!" I said, outloud this time, suddenly knowing my mother wouldn't be terribly reasonable about all this, and then horror of horrors, realizing too, that I might be invoking the wrath of that crazy woman, Tante Nuht. In my rising fear all I could see was a bloody cleaver and a swinging baseball bat. I had made a mistake. A big mistake. I knew as a kid knows something for sure that if Tante Nuht ever got a hold of me, I would never survive. I knew then that I would never unlock the door.

My dad, as always, tried reasoning with me to raise the lock knob. I just watched as Tante Nuht walked round and round the car, muttering and threatening.

I can't remember how they finally got in. I think Dad wedged his hand in through the little triangular vent window at the front of the door, but it's all a little fuzzy now. It must be that the terror I went through realizing I had made myself an enemy of Tante Nuht has hidden itself deep in my suppressed memory.

Tante Nuht stands in my family's memory as a terrible but wonderful person. While we always knew to stay just out of range of whatever her weapon of the day was, we loved this woman. We were awed by her; we were amazed by her; we were captivated by her zestiness, her enthusiasm, her creativity.

I don't know where the tradition that God is a slow-moving serious old man comes from. I think there's good evidence in Scripture and in observing creation that the feistiness, the love of life, the attractiveness that we saw in Tante Nuht rubbed off of God somehow. While we do tend to keep our distance from God–to get too close would mean we might get awed to death–there is so much about God that makes us gravitate towards him, wanting to just be close and in the vicinity all the time.

Tante Nuht had an infectious spirit; God is the infectious Spirit. Tante Nuht was outrageous in her behavior; God is outrageous in how he loves us, sent his Son to save us, sends his Spirit to help us. When I

see the God who made Tante Nuht, I want to travel
with him, anywhere, anytime, and love him, all the
while being just a little bit afraid. I am not wise
enough to know what his next move may be, but I do
hope to see him make it.

Tante
Nuht

Mom

The steps curved around, not because the house was so big, but because it was so small. A curved stairway was the best way to use up the corner from the kitchen to the bedrooms upstairs. The wooden stairs were protected from wear in the center by rectangular remnants of linoleum scavenged from when the living room floor was re-done. The lino might have protected the step landings, but they didn't protect young boys in sock feet.

I slipped about two steps from the top, coming down at high speed one day, and fell down the next seven or eight stairs. I crashed through the door, three steps above the kitchen floor, snapping off the latch that held the door closed, and landed in a heap on the kitchen floor. My mother, two quick steps from my crash landing site, was terrified. Terrified that I might have seriously injured myself; terrified that I might be permanently injured; terrified by the sheer noise and bedlam exploding into the hum of her kitchen warmth and peace. In her horror and her fear, she struck me a glancing blow on the head and screamed, "Why aren't you careful. You could have hurt yourself." Even in my little boy's mind, I wondered how she could truly worry about me hurting myself in a fall, when it didn't seem to register in her mind that she was hurting me with her hitting. I never forgot.

I grew up and mother became a calmer person. I learned in my growing up that mother had had too many children, too many physical ailments, too much work, too few dreams realized, and too few rewards from life. And she was often ill. Ill so often, our usual response to the latest ailment was passivity and less compassion. But finally she was sick, really sick, and dying. And when we knew for sure that she was really dying, we did give her the attention she needed, and we learned to care for her.

She had a blood disease. Between weekly blood transfusions, a curious kind of muscle massing often occurred in regions of her back that caused excruciating pain, even over substantial doses of morphine. The only solution, discovered by Dad, was to reach a fist under the blanket and through the so often infuriating opening in the hospital gown and under mother's back, her own weight pushing the moving fist into the bed. By moving his hand around, Dad learned to find the spastic muscle mass causing the pain, and by thrusting his flat fist up into the pain, the mass was discharged and the pain released. He relieved her from her pain dozens and possibly hundreds of times in the last six months of life with his discovery.

I drove the three hours out to the country hospital to visit my mom one day close to the end to relieve my dad a bit, and hopefully, care for Mom a little after years of more or less ignoring her constantly-talked-about ailments. I sincerely wished to encourage them both.

I arrived at the hospital early in the afternoon and I think Dad wanted the three of us to stay for a while. Seeing the tiredness around his eyes and the fading tan on his golf-loving face, I sent him home. "Go home, Dad," I said, "take a break!" He left with a sad stoop, realizing a break was desperately needed, but still sure he was abandoning something, someone.

Mother rested, her eyes closed. Her existence was morphine-rich. She drifted in and out of sleep and wakefulness. "You want to talk?" she asked.

"Yeah!" I guessed outloud, though I was surprised at the question.

"About us? You and me?" she asked, though it seemed hardly a question. Her eyes started open, wild. The pain was suddenly kicking through the drugs. She reached over the side of the bed and grabbed my hand. She pulled it over the safety bar and shoved it under her back. I pulled back, looking for eyes to tell me it was really all right for me, her son, to touch her this way. I had not touched her skin ever except her hands, her face, in quick kisses, and quick touches. I had too often felt smothered, had needed always to get away. She didn't care about all that today, and this woman, this mother of mine, who had tried to protect me from the misuse of sexuality by largely denying its very existence, was now guiding my hand across her own soft skin down around her lower back, seeking the killing pain, the mass of excruciating pressure. I tried once more to pull away my hand, taboo bells ringing and screaming in my head. She pulled my hand around the kidneys, groping, searching.

"There! There! You've found it," she squealed. "Push your fist up against the weight of my body," she hissed through clinched teeth.

I felt the mass, I felt it give way and spread out, flattened from the pressure I had been able to exert on it. Mother groaned and sighed, "You don't know how that feels! You don't know how good that feels!"

I withdrew my hand. Tucked the blankets around her. She opened her eyes and smiled. "Thanks!" she said, "Thanks!"

Tears filled my eyes for the second time that day. Not an hour earlier she had said, "For hitting you, when you were younger, I'm sorry!"

Suddenly now that I was able to give my mom relief, so much physical pleasure in massaging out the hellish pain in her back, I realized that I had completed the circle of pleasure and pain, violence and kindness. Without premeditation, I had unwittingly met her physical cruelty of me in my childhood with physical comforting in my adulthood.

And the score was settled. I knew in that second that the thing was done. Forgiveness and finishedness rolled in waves through my being. I held her for a long time, stroked her hair, and said, "I love you, Mom!" for the first time in my memory, believing it. For the first time feeling I could safely say it without feeling compelled to do so, or without feeling I was just setting myself up for more smothering.

"I love you, Mom!" with no agenda, just the love of a grown child for his parent, is a wonderful thing. But I said it and I meant it. I experienced it.

The next time I saw her, she lay in her coffin. I weep and I smile as I remember that last "clearing" we had. It was like a thousand clearings. It lives on. And we are clean, my mom and I. And we are finished. It was, it is, over. My, what a good finish that was.

Forgiveness. Is it a word or just an idea? Is it explainable? How does one get it? I think it's more an ongoing thing than the utterance of some special words just once, this forgiveness.

I wasn't even looking for a cleaning of the slate, a forgiveness, with my mom in the hospital that day. I was just doing the duty of an adult child for a dying parent. If you would have asked me what part ritual plays in serving up meaning to the experience of forgiveness, I would have stared at you blankly. Forgiveness, I would have thought, is the words, "I forgive you!" Now I know that these words are only the beginning, or maybe just the ending. The articulation of forgiveness comes in the words, but the experience of forgiveness comes in the act, the touch, the relief both in body and in spirit.

When the nails went through the sinew of God's hands, when the spear went into his soft fleshy side, the horror of sin and condemnation must have burned like hell, but when the spirit rose out of the body, the relief, the release, the deliverance must have been like songs in a jail, like water in a desert, like food to the starving, like a check to the unemployed, only better. I can't grasp how Jesus' soul must have soared when his spirit rose up; but my informed imagination tells me it was a rise-up beyond every soaring I've ever had, and I lean towards it. To fly with Jesus, to run with God, is and will be better than anything. He is the epitome, the personification, the divination of forgiveness. He takes it all, our angry words, our killing deeds, our abusive acts, our vandalous behavior, and he cleans it all up. And he keeps the time-released cleanliness going forever.

I imagine Jesus taking my face in his hands and, looking straight into my eyes, saying, "I forgive you! I forgive you!" I don't know whether to click my heels or fall down weeping. They are both appropriate, for I am forgiven. I am forgiven everything!

Mom

Jacob

y dad, Jacob, never took me fishing. He never took me to an NHL hockey game. He never took me to Disneyland. And he never took me on a father-and-son camping trip. He didn't need to. We must have fenced a thousand miles of pastureland together, and we probably traveled a hundred thousand miles together in the truck, hauling grain, taking cattle to the auction, or getting the bull from the neighbors.

I don't know if he ever set out to teach me anything. He just talked, and he talked a lot. He talked about growing up in a Russian Mennonite village. He talked about the beautiful Motherland; he ached for her beauty and her rich Siberian soil. I think he harbored a sadness for having had to leave Russia as he did with his parents in the late 1920's. Dad would have preferred to have stayed there, if it were not for the social, economic, political, and spiritual desert that Russia entered with the Revolution. Despite his warm memories and near familial bond to Mother Russia, Dad daily gave thanks for the safety and the goodness and the opportunity of Canada.

In his telling, Dad talked about not having been able to get an education past Grade 6, and he marveled how he came to be chairman of the local School Board, setting policies, hiring teachers, and generally leading and helping to ensure the education of his own children and the kids of the community.

I farmed with my dad all those growing up years, and I soon noticed that he would rather help the neighbors than learn the art of farming himself; he

109

would rather visit with relatives from far away than
harrow the back forty. But he worked hard, too
hard, and became moderately successful without
ever uttering a complaint or a wish that he could be
doing something else. Only after he was comfort-
ably retired and deeply ensconced in volunteer work
and golfing did he tell us he had never wanted to be
a farmer. He had felt he had no choice; he would
have much rather been a pharmacist or a doctor
with all the education it takes to be such.

Dad was a devout man. His faith exercised itself
in common sense, calmness, and serenity, and in a
deep love for people that caused others to respect
and like him in return.

Dad's German-accented English carried no oaths
or swear words. He never swore. Except once.
Dad, my brother, and I were cleaning the barn one
Saturday. One of our thousand-pound steers, roam-
ing loosely around the barn, must have stepped on
Dad's rubber-booted toe, or flicked him in the eye
with a coarse manure-coated tail. And Dad lost it.
Having never seen him angry before, and only once
more since, my brother and I were astonished as
Dad struck the beast a terrific wallop with the long
handle of a barn fork. And as he swung the handle
he shouted the ineffable "S" word, the word that
really describes what was all over the floor of the
barn. My brother and I covered our mouths with
mittened hands, nearly exploding with amazement
and delight that our dad had said a "bad word."
Carefully avoiding eye contact with us, Dad went
back to his quiet work after his singular and explo-
sive outburst of angry passion, as the steer stood in
the corner twitching its tail. My brother and I scurried along the far side of the center barn aisle, scoot-
ed out the barn door, and raced the hundred meters
to the house along the narrow-grooved path in the
snow, shiny white with frost and flecked with
brownish barn stains we thought we now had per-

mission to call by its right name. Slamming through the house door, we repeated over and over, with sparkly-eyed delight, and to our poor mother's horror, the favorite word of the day. After all, if Dad used it, so could we. Dad came to the house a half hour later, a little sheepish grin on his face. I wonder how he guessed we were quoting him all over the place.

Dad was a quietly stubborn man. He didn't argue or fight back very often. He just quietly puttered about, refusing to be pushed around.

On those exceedingly rare mornings of our childhood when we kids understood that we were leaving on a legendary visit to our grandparents and cousins three days drive away, Dad was cool. About the time that Mom had bathed us and dressed us for the trip, and we thought it was nearly time to get into the car, Dad would pick up his hammer and a Rogers Golden Corn Syrup pail full of fencing nails and head out to the pasture.

"Where are you going, Dad?" we kids would yell out after him. "Aren't we leaving for B.C.?"

""Who's going to keep the cows in the fence when we're all gone if the fence needs fixing?" he'd call out. "You people don't have to think of those things!"

An hour later he came shuffling back to the house, and then to our mother's horror, he would place a few two by ten planks and a couple of wooden blocks in front of the front tires of the car, and nose the car up his homemade ramp.

"What are you doin' now?" we would scream. "Changin' the oil," he said, "You don't expect this car to go all the way to B.C. with dirty oil, do you?"

"Well, why didn't you change the oil before?" some smart-mouthed kid would ask.

"Cause I was fixing the fence," he'd answer.

After the oil change, one of us would have to hold the tape measure from tire to tire as he made sure the front wheels were properly aligned. We usually left for B.C. on these semi-annual trips by mid-afternoon of the day the rest of us had thought we had planned to leave first thing in the morning. The first few miles were always quiet.

Though gentle and unauthoritarian, Dad set a conduct standard for us that was unconfused. Immigrant Mennonite teenagers in our community soon learned that though God does not gradate sins, the worst thing one could do was go to a dance at the high school. More important things, such as those of a sexual nature, were never mentioned, as if the sex-drive were nonexistent or too sacred to talk about. As a result, most of us Mennonite kids did not attend dances, though we did spend many weekend evenings in the back seats of our dads' cars parked on "lovers lane" east of town because we had never been told not to do that.

One Friday night, probably unconsciously testing whether I was being allowed to grow up and make some of my own decisions, I asked Dad if I could have the car to "go to the dance!" Dad stood up from under the deep-tiller on which he was changing the shovels, reached in his pocket, gave me the car keys, and asked, "Can you?"

I went to the dance. It was awful. Only the girls danced, all together in a bunch in the middle of the darkened gym, or went to the washroom in that same bunch, like hiving bees, while the boys stood around the edges of the gym trying to look cool in whatever ways looked cool that year, and never went to the washroom. Did Dad know that these events would be this goofy, this wooden?

I was at a meeting last week in California. We were sitting in a board room with large French doors that opened into a reception and receiving area. I looked up from my papers and out into the reception area through the closed glass doors. At the counter stood an elderly man, grey-coated and grey-capped, looking like he was asking for someone, looking for someone. I started to my feet, shocked to see this incredibly familiar looking man, my dad, way down here in California, completely having forgotten that he had died last year. Instantly remembering his death, however, I sat back down, tears filling my eyes, again. The meeting around me continued as I remembered his rough red stubbly beard that scraped me when we hugged. I remembered that unusual and unique smell of his skin that had remained reminiscent of the shaving cream soap and cup, exchanged for the electric machine years ago, that hung about his being.

Dad was a good man. An incredibly good man. When we were kids playing hockey, he always came into the dressing room between periods and gave each kid a stick of gum.

But I remember him lying to me once. I had not yet started school and loved to go to town with him on those very few occasions when he went for business. I learned early, though, that he often left me at home from those trips to town, because leaving me crying at home was easier than letting me come along and disappointing me with not having a nickel or even a few pennies for some candies or a jawbreaker.

One day, however, he found me playing somewhere in the yard and most enthusiastically asked if I wanted to go to town. "Yes!" I beamed, thinking a little boy's heaven must be at hand. I crawled up into our green '52 Ford car with the green-and-white plastic plaid seat covers and stood on the seat beside him with one hand on his shoulder as he drove. He turned south, and even my four-year-old mind registered that this was not the way to town. At the next mile, Dad turned the car west toward the school where my brother and sisters went. "Perhaps he was taking them along to town, too," I thought. We turned into the schoolyard, pulled up, and parked beside a car parked on the gravel patch beside the school. It was odd that another car stood in the schoolyard, I remember now, because our school teachers, young and inexperienced and teaching on letters of permit, could never afford cars of their own.

"Let's go in!" he said. By now I was mystified. Dad took my hand safely in his and he waited as I stepped carefully, little boy style, up the cracked concrete steps and into the porch of the one-roomed school. The porch, which doubled as a cloak and mud room, smelled of the wet clothes, farm kids' boots, and the school kids themselves, and through the open door wafted that strange odor of oiled floor that one only smelled in schools. As Dad helped me take off my jacket I could see the picture of the new Queen at the front of the class-room above the row of written and printed alphabet letters, white on green, above the blackboard. I could hear kids talking, and I could make out the familiar voices of my brother and two of my sisters, and my cousins, and the other neighborhood kids I knew.

I was, by this time, awfully curious as to what was going on. This was all strange, coming to school with my dad when he had invited me to town.

As we entered the room I could see the pupils of the school, all 15 or 16 of them, ranging from Grade 1 to Grade 9 correspondence, lined up in a row from largest to smallest with one shirt sleeve rolled up high on their arms. At the head of the line stood the teacher, and just behind her stood a white coated gentleman, Dr. Roy. I knew him. In that second of realization, I could see Dr. Roy holding up what looked like a mammoth syringe with a small bottle poised upside-down on the end of that syringe. Slowly he pulled down the little handle, filling the syringe. I started to scream and tried to twist around my dad's legs and head for the door.

He picked me up in his strong arms and we moved toward the good doctor.

I don't remember how long I screamed after the needle that I was sure was itself twice as big as I was, but I think the screaming lasted quite some time past when we were all safely home again. I'm not sure, though, that the screaming was all about the horror of needles and doctors and such unpleasantries; it was probably a scream against the new awareness that dads aren't perfect. I don't remember whether Dad ever asked me if I wanted to go to town again.

Dad always said, in his later years, that he wanted to die fast, on the golf course or in church. He played 36 holes of golf one day in August last year after a few months of angina pain that he was sure he could mend with a little Vick's VaporRub. By evening of the 36 holes, he was more tired than usual for an 82-year-old and even, amazingly, suggested himself that he be taken to the emergency ward. He did have a heart attack of some magnitude, but after three days he was talking about golfing again, and "getting out of here!" I talked to him on the phone on the third day after the attack. He was feeling strong. "Ready to go!" he said.

"I love you, Dad!" I said, and I choked. He let it go past him, though he had said it to me as often as I to him, probably sensing my emotion as being too much to handle that day.

The next morning they phoned me. "He got up to go to the bathroom and fell down dead," they said.

I still love my dad, Old Jake, easily as much today as I did when he was still alive. I hope he smiled sometime in that last day, knowing I loved him; I always knew he loved me.

The strongest metaphor for God in the Bible is probably God as Father. But never can we get stuck on God being just a big version of our own earthly father, no matter how good he was, nor certainly how bad. If my children are limited in their view of God by their impressions of me, their dad, they will always come short on encountering God as he is.

I weep for those people in our congregations who cannot hear us refer to "Father God" because their experience of father has been so horrific, not only because they never had the father they deserved to have, but because they have been unable to let God as he lovingly is shine into their broken and hungry hearts.

I never spent a moment wondering whether my dad loved me, nor did I ever wonder whether he thought I was anything but special. That I never wondered about my dad and me means that I never needed to spend much time wondering about me. As a result, perhaps, I never doubt that God doesn't see me as anything but a special child of his who will get all the affectionate love and compassionate care I need.

I was blessed with a dad who gave me the experience of knowing I am loved and then, by extension, the ability to know that God is thousands, no, millions of times more understanding, cool-headed, caring, wise, friendly, outgoing, interested, and steady than my dad was. Beyond that, I live in the biblical reinforcement of those perceptions, and I also know that he, my Father God, will never leave me nor forsake me.

I will not sit on God's grave and cry at his absence as I have on my dad's. He, my Father God, is always here with us, beside us, before us, behind us, above us.

What was stubbornness in my dad, is faithfulness in my Father; what was manipulation in my dad to get a kid inoculated, is power and truth in my Father.

The ache in my heart to talk to my dad about the weather and the curling bonspiel on TV is really the ache in all our hearts for God who engendered us, created us, who parents us, and who nurtures us forever.

Until we come to know that God is the best Father we can dream of or imagine, multiplied a thousand and a million times over, we live orphaned. But we are not orphans. We have a Father. And he is God.

Jacob